The Alcoholism Handbook

A Positive and Effective Recovery Plan for You and Yours

A Progressive Look into Alcoholism with Special Emphasis on Treatment, Recovery, and Long-Term Maintenance for the Drinking Person and His or Her Family.

Greg Robinson

authorHOUSE®

AuthorHouse™
1663 Liberty Drive
Bloomington, IN 47403
www.authorhouse.com
Phone: 1 (800) 839-8640

Published by AuthorHouse 10/13/2017

ISBN: 978-1-5462-1151-8 (sc)
ISBN: 978-1-5462-1152-5 (hc)
ISBN: 978-1-5462-1150-1 (e)

Library of Congress Control Number: 2017915352

Print information available on the last page.

Disclaimer

This book is not to be used or substituted without consultation with your medical doctor, physician, or professional counselor, psychiatrist, or psychologist. The author, publisher, and/or experts specifically listed in this publication aren't responsible for any consequences, direct or indirect, resulting from the readers' actions. All recommended supplements, vitamins, minerals, herbs, and dosages are recommended ranges for healthy individuals, and each person is different as to tolerance levels and allergic reactions. The reader of this book is instructed to consult with his or her personal physician before starting a program of supplements suggested in this book. If you are taking medications, consult with your physician before starting a supplement program because there are adverse effects with some medications and supplements. The purpose of this book is to educate the reader with knowledge and awareness of alcoholism and the use of nutrition and supplements in the enhancement of the person's health if he or she has long-term alcohol use or abuse. Abuse of alcohol is defined as more than one drink, one ounce of alcohol per day.

The author of this book doesn't dispense medical advice or prescribe the use of any technique as a form of treatment for physical, emotional, or medical problems without the advice of a physician, either directly or indirectly. The intent of the author is only to offer information and awareness of a general nature to help you in your quest for emotional, physical, and spiritual well-being. In the event that you use any of the information in this book for yourself, the author and publisher assume no responsibility for your actions.

Dear Reader,

As a Community Resource Manager for the Department of Corrections and Rehabilitation, with over 15 years of experience working hand in hand with numerous self-help programs and the literature that corresponds with these programs, it is my pleasure to highly recommend "The Alcoholism Handbook". This comprehensive book about alcoholism, and most importantly recovery, is a learning tool as well as a teaching tool that could easily be incorporated into the current literature used in treatment centers, hospitals, health care facilities, and prisons.

This book could also be used as an excellent teaching tool for law enforcement, or the legal system in dealing with the consequences of alcoholic behaviors. As somebody who has used many different reading materials to help the alcoholic who still suffers I can see this book also being helpful to all clinicians who may be searching for a more in depth understanding of the disease of alcoholism and the recovery process that must take place for the alcoholic to get, and stay sober.

The knowledge and experience of the author really come through in each chapter. The book is a big picture overview of alcoholism and recovery and covers many areas, such as nutrition, that I have not seen in any other literature. This book provides a treatment plan that is positive and will help any person who wants it. I do believe that this book could save many lives. Every judge, lawyer, social, worker, nurse, physician, and family who come into contact with alcoholics should access the tools available to them in "The Alcoholism Handbook" and use these tools as intended, a positive and progressive approach to the treatment or prevention of alcoholism.

Sincerely,

Bill Parker

I was so impressed with *The Alcoholism Handbook's* approach to treatment recovery, and long-term maintenance. The positive lifestyle changes approach with the use of vitamin supplements is a positive approach to the treatment of the disease. This book is comprehensive and would be an excellent tool for teaching or learning.

As a Program Manager at a Mental Health facility for eighteen years, I am familiar with the indirect consequences of alcohol and alcoholism. I was involved with Fetal Alcohol Syndrome, in children from a young age to adolescents, and the extreme mental retardation is devastating. The consequences of drinking alcohol while pregnant are incomprehensible. The life-long consequences to the child, adolescent, adult child, and mother are indescribable, and last a lifetime.

The Alcoholism Handbook is a fantastic overview of alcoholism, from the treatment to the recovery of the disease. The author's experience and expertise in this area is well communicated in every chapter.

As a program manager, I have reviewed a lot of teaching material to be used in the mental health facility, and *The Alcoholism Handbook* is a complete overview of the disease, treatment, and recovery of alcoholism. This reading would be a great reference and teaching tool for all social or legal agencies dealing with the aftermath of alcohol. It would benefit greatly prenatal classes, and nursing programs. It would be an exceptional training tool in colleges, universities, nursing programs, prisons, and treatment centers, or for anyone dealing directly with the consequences of alcohol. I believe this book can provide a non-drinking lifestyle for people where alcohol is causing problems, or the alcoholic. *The Alcoholism Handbook* can save many lives.

Sincerely,

Ralph Seitz

This book is dedicated to the alcoholic who still suffers. I dedicate this book to you, the alcoholic, the family member, and everyone else directly or indirectly affected by the consequences of alcohol.

I acknowledge and thank my higher power, God, in the writing of this book.

This book is written to save another life.

I provide an in-depth look into alcoholism and offer a positive and progressive approach to the treatment, recovery, and long-term maintenance of the disease for the alcoholic and his or her family. The reader will also learn a plan to return to health that includes the use of nutrition and vitamin supplements for wellness. *The Alcoholism Handbook* will save the life of an alcoholic and heal his or her family members.

I give an overview of alcohol addiction, treatment, recovery, and the lifetime maintenance of the disease. Alcoholism can be suppressed if the alcoholic is willing to learn something new and has a desire to stop drinking. The tools provided in this book are needed to overcome this devastating disease. Alcohol use affects many people in some way, whether directly or indirectly. Watching a parent, friend, son or daughter, family member, or coworker struggle with this disease is incomprehensibly disturbing. With this book, the tools provided, and the grace of God, pray for the alcoholic and a miracle. Most every alcoholic can become one of those miracles if they want to.

The Alcoholism Handbook will also help you, the reader, transition to a positive-living lifestyle for the alcoholic and his or her family. It will provide you the necessary steps to achieve a nondrinking lifestyle and find peace of mind.

The suggestions and general protocol I present can also be applied to any other addiction, including drugs, opioids, sex, overeating, smoking, gambling, or marijuana. With more legalization of marijuana in many states, the information in this book may now be applied to the substance abuse of marijuana. Many of the same consequences of alcohol addiction will materialize in a population where marijuana is used as a social and medicinal drug.

Addiction is about what you are using, and why you are using it.

If Alcohol is causing you problems, then alcohol *is* the problem.

–Anonymous

Table of Contents

Acknowledgments

This book is written with love and appreciation to my children who have unknowingly supported me in my efforts and helped keep me grounded. I thank my children for letting me be their teacher in life, about life, and for life. At the same time I'm grateful for their teaching me and refreshing my memory on the basic values of life. I thank my children for their support, understanding, and encouragement.

Here's a special acknowledgment and loving appreciation for my wife, Rosalie, for her presence, which God has blessed me with, for believing in me, and for providing me with inspiration and the greatest desire to be the best I can be. Her pure innocence, knowledge, religious teachings, and trust of me remind me of what life is all about and of the purpose God has for me. She provides me inspiration for doing the right things in life. Her educational questions and her loyalty have helped teach me unconditional love. I'm thankful for the inspiration she has given me, her trust of my knowledge, and her eagerness and willingness to listen, practice, and learn from each other. Rosalie has truly been a gift from God. I thank her for allowing me to be her teacher in life, her mentor, and her friend. She has been my friend, for which I am most grateful.

This book is written with the mentoring support of Dr. Allan Hedberg, PhD, clinical and consulting psychologist. A special thanks to Dr. Hedberg for his input, expertise, and understanding of human nature and the disease of alcoholism. Dr. Hedberg has been a great mentor and inspiration for me. I want to acknowledge and thank him and his staff for their in-depth input and countless hours of review, and for his knowledge, support, and expertise in the writing of this book.

I would also like to give a special tribute to Phyllis Balch, CNC, and James Balch, MD, for their book *Prescription for Nutritional Healing*. Their book is one of the greatest books I have read in dealing with natural health, vitamins, minerals, herbs, and nutritional healing. I give a special acknowledgment to Dr. Gary Null and his outstanding books and teachings on natural medicine, nutrition, anti-aging, vitamins, minerals, and herbs.

I want to acknowledge the writings of Bill W. and the Alcoholics Anonymous program for all the lifesaving information available in that program. This is one of the most successful and beneficial programs I have ever encountered. AA teaches a program for living and provides a wealth of lifesaving information for the alcoholic. It has been around since the 1930s and has a current membership of two million plus. It is unsurpassed in its benefits and the number of lives and families it has saved.

For a detailed analysis of a journey into alcoholism and a detailed step-by-step process into recovery, I recommend the book *The Longest Trek: My Tour of the Galaxy* by Grace Lee Whitney (Quill Driver Publishing, 1998). You may know Grace as Yeoman Janice Rand from the original Star Trek series. Grace was an actress, entertainer, and singer; and her book encompasses the disease of alcoholism and describes her recovery in detail. She analyzes her lifelong experience and detailed recovery from alcoholism through AA's twelve-step program. Grace (1930–2015) lives on through her book and movies.

Introduction

Alcohol is a worldwide phenomenon that is socially acceptable and legal in every way. With some age restrictions and special licensing, alcohol is normally available to anyone over the age of twenty-one. It is associated with going to parties and weddings, having fun, talking, being social, celebrating, and being accepted. But every drink of alcohol that is more than one for certain individuals brings the subtle destruction of morals and values; one's mind, body, and spirit; and one's thinking ability.

Numerous endorsements and advertisements state that one drink, one ounce of alcohol per day is good for stress and heart health. I believe those endorsements, but this book is written for the person who cannot drink just one drink. Alcoholism is progressive, and many times for many individuals, one drink leads to two, two drinks lead to three, and three drinks lead to four or more. Then all the beneficial effects of alcohol are lost. I assure you that every alcoholic started out drinking only one to two drinks.

Alcohol use is on the rise in women, children, teenagers, and college students. It is a normal part of many lives, but alcohol is subtle and progressive, and it can be deadly. Alcohol is a liquid that has little to no nutritional qualities and may become hazardous to one's own health and well-being—and is oh so subtle.

Alcoholism is a personal disease. Alcoholism can be arrested, subdued, and quieted; but the disease can never be cured, and it does not go away. I compare alcoholism to cancer; you can use chemotherapy or radiation to remove the cancer, but the cancer may return at any time. For alcoholism, you may use a positive-living program to remove and arrest the desire to drink, but the disease is always there, waiting to come back in full force.

Some alcoholics may stop drinking on their own, but they are still the same people and have the same personality traits they did when drinking. They haven't changed their lives, thinking, or lifestyles. With this recovery program, you will learn a new way to live; a nondrinking lifestyle.

The Alcoholism Handbook will provide all the necessary steps to achieve a nondrinking lifestyle and peace of mind.

The rise of independence in women started in the 1950s and continues to the present. With all the equality women wanted, now they get the equality of alcoholism. Women are now full partners in this disease. In the year 2017, deciding to work and have a career is no longer an equality or independence issue. It is essential; it is a goal of many women. And with that equality, there is an equal share of alcoholism.

The Alcoholism Handbook is written for those people who do destructive things to themselves through drinking alcohol and don't know why. This book is for those people who know something is wrong but don't know what. It is written for people who have an alcohol problem, the potential alcoholic, and anyone drinking alcohol who cannot stop. It is written for the person for whom alcohol is causing problems. It is for those who drink alcohol daily, drink from party to party, or drink days and weeks at a time and then stop for a long period, only to do so again later.

This book is for the person who thinks of having another drink, a person who cannot drink half a drink and walk away. It is for the person for whom alcohol is causing problems; then alcohol *is* the problem. If alcohol is causing you problems in health, finance, relationships, or work, then this book is for you and your family. It is for those who have received their first DUI or for the drinking person who has had a divorce, lost his or her job, passed out and doesn't remember what happened, or hurt himself or herself or others because of drinking.

This book is for the person who still suffers. These writings are meant to be suggestive only. Alcoholics work and function best by suggestion. The alcoholic, maybe for the first time, now will have a choice to open his or her mind a little and learn a different way of living. Or the person may put this book down and continue on with the way he or she is currently living. Ask yourself, is alcohol causing you or your family members problems?

The Alcoholism Handbook is also written for treatment centers, physicians, clergymen, professional health care personnel, psychiatrists, psychologists, counselors, judges, law enforcement personnel, and social workers. It is also intended for a nondrinking spouse and family members, whose lives alcohol has touched in some negative way, either directly or indirectly. The intent of this book is to give you an in-depth awareness into alcoholic thinking, treatment, recovery, and long-term maintenance. This book is also written for the caregiver, spouse, family member, and anyone who is unknowingly enabling the alcoholic to drink.

The Alcoholism Handbook will also introduce you, the reader, to a step-by-step process to transition to a positive living lifestyle. It will provide the steps necessary to achieve a nondrinking lifestyle. The intent of this book is to provide an in-depth look at an alcoholic, including his or her experience, strength, and hope. It will point you toward the program of Alcoholics Anonymous and the twelve steps that have helped so many people with a drinking problem. I don't intend to take anything from the twelve steps of Alcoholics Anonymous, but I desire only to enhance, clarify, and provide an in-depth look into the life of an alcoholic, a recovery program, and a lifestyle that will allow him or her to become whole again as a positive, functioning member of society and a loving spouse or parent.

The programs and suggestions presented here aren't a replacement for the twelve-step program of Alcoholics Anonymous; there are many paths to recovery. What I present is intended to clearly demonstrate the symptoms, consequences, treatment, recovery, and long-term maintenance from alcoholism. It is also intended to promote hope if you or a loved one suffers from this disease either directly or indirectly. A recovery program will show you the way toward a lifestyle that centers on the positive aspects of life lived free of alcohol and the profound peace and happiness that results from the choice of sobriety. *The Alcoholism*

Handbook will show you, your spouse, and family how to be whole again with a respectful, loving relationship. It will help alcoholics understand that, for the first time in years, they have the choice to drink or not to drink and to enhance their mind, body, and spirit.

Chapter 1

What Is Alcoholism?

Alcoholism is a disease of the mind, body, and spirit. Alcohol is the fermented sugary liquid from certain fruits, grains, or vegetables that, when distilled correctly, produces a gas. When the gas is cooled, it produces a liquid referred to as alcohol. Alcohol isn't a mystery. It has been around for centuries; it is a feel-good liquid that allows people to let down their inhibitions and boundaries, and lose their common sense, judgment, morals, and beliefs. It allows them to be free and to be what they are not.

Alcohol takes the mind to a place where everything is good and there are no problems. It gives drinkers a warm and fuzzy feeling, but every drink they take brings a subtle destruction of values, life, mind, body, spirit, dignity, and thinking ability. Alcoholism is so subtle that they don't even notice the change. If you're a normal drinker who can take only one drink and stop, drink half a drink and walk away, or drink only once or twice a year, I admire you. For the alcoholic, who loves alcohol and is addicted to it, one drink is too much, and twenty drinks are never enough.

Alcoholism is a slow, subtle, progressive disease. Unlike cancer, a physical disease of the body, alcoholism destroys the mind, body, and spirit. It cannot be cured, only suppressed. There are no prescriptions, medications, pills, vaccines, or shots; nothing will cure alcoholism. People can hold the disease in abeyance, in suspension, but they can't get rid of it. For the alcoholic, the desire for a drink will never completely go away. Alcoholism, like cancer, is a slow, subtle, agonizing death. It's like a roller coaster; the upside feels so good, but the downside becomes steeper and steeper and lasts longer and longer—until at some point in time, there is no more upside.

1

Drinking usually starts out as a social behavior, whether someone watched his or her parents drink or got in a social situation where everyone else was doing it, so he or she tried it. Many people can stop, but some cannot. As the drinking continues, it is very subtle because every once in a while, a little more is required to get that same good feeling. No alcoholic ever starts out thinking, *I will have one drink, and then I'll be an alcoholic.* The thinking is quite the opposite: *I can have one drink, or I can have ten. I am still in control of myself.* Alcoholics will claim to the last day of their drinking that they are in control of themselves; they think they are in control of the alcohol. It is only when they admit they aren't in control that the situation can get better.

Alcoholics try many times to stop drinking, but a tremendous fear sets in every time they get the thought that they want to stop. A true alcoholic doesn't know how to function without alcohol. He or she cannot comprehend living without a drink during his or her acceptable habitual drinking time, whether it is daily, weekly, monthly, during binge drinking, or just during parties. Whatever pattern they have set they will follow time and time again, with one exception; the amount of time spent drinking and the amount consumed will increase. This is a guaranteed fact of every alcoholic. This is tolerance building, and it shows the progressive nature of the disease. Alcoholism gets worse but never gets better.

Alcohol probably exceeds cancer in destruction, because alcohol affects not only individuals but also families, children, relatives, workplaces, and other people who are killed or injured by drunk drivers. Cancer, on one hand, affects the individual and indirectly the family. Alcohol directly affects individuals and their family. Take note of the destruction and mushrooming effect from the impact of alcohol. The fact is that alcohol is everywhere. Alcoholism cures aren't the same as cancer or other deadly diseases. Here is the difference; alcoholism is the only known disease from which the individual derives pleasure. In no other disease is there pleasure derived from it. Alcohol, on the other hand, is consumed *because* of the pleasure, not the pain. The pain is secondary in nature to the alcoholic because it comes only occasionally. The more years or decades of drinking that take place, the more pain will increase at a subtle but progressive pace.

Alcoholism is the inability to drink only one drink. Once the "ism" sets in, an alcoholic cannot stop drinking—and no alcoholic can ever tell you when that "ism" sets in. Alcoholism defies any help and won't seek help; it will always tell the person to have another drink—just have another drink, and that will fix the problem. For any other disease, flu, or pain, the person will go to a doctor. But alcoholism is so subtle and strong that it defies any help or suggestions of help. Jail, DUIs (driving-under-the-influence citations), divorces, job loss, bankruptcy, hospitalization, or incomprehensible demoralization won't stop the disease. The answer is always to have another drink. Once alcoholism sets in, an alcoholic can stop drinking only by the grace of God with some type of intervention, some drastic life event, something so horrible that it wakes the alcoholic up, or some internal choice for hope and change.

Alcoholics are usually self-centered to the extreme; everything, especially the alcohol, is about them. They have a million reasons to drink and not one reason to stop.

Alcoholics generally have anger and guilt issues from the past, and these feelings may be subtly exaggerated over time, because they can no longer control the alcohol. They have self-esteem issues and denied feelings of failure, and a great number of alcoholics I have talked to are what is referred to as "spiritually deficient." Many alcoholics generally lack God or a higher power, and they may not practice any religious teachings. Inadvertently they may subtly choose alcohol as their main priority, the greatest thing in their lives. Many make alcohol their spiritual power in their lives. In a short period of time, the alcohol is in control, but the alcoholic will never admit this. Sometimes for years, decades, or even many decades, many will never admit it, even into death. Many will pursue alcohol into hospitals, treatment centers, divorces, bankruptcies, jails, insanity, or death.

Alcoholism is a subtle lubricant for self-destructive and negative thinking. It tells people they can have another drink, that they must have another drink but that they should never, ever ask for help.

A certain percentage of the population, once they taste alcohol and feel the effect, will continue to drink until death. These are alcoholics. They put alcohol above everything else, including spouse, job, career, children, and even life itself. They are obsessed with alcohol and will do or say anything to get it. Alcoholism, in my opinion, is the number one contributor to the destruction of families, especially those with children, and to divorces in this country. It is a major contributor to dysfunction in families and the workplace. Alcohol-related diseases are numerous, and the number of deaths attributable to them is great. A death certificate will always show a physical cause, such as liver failure or heart failure, but it will never show that too much alcohol caused the death. Some diseases blatantly associated with alcoholism are cirrhosis of the liver, kidney failure, diabetes, and numerous heart problems related to an enlarged heart, including high blood pressure and stroke. Despite its familiarity and long history, alcoholism is still one of the mysteries of the universe. As a mental obsession, alcoholism is a disease of the mind; as a physical dependence it is a disease of the body. As alcohol strips away a person's morals, values, spirituality, and religious beliefs, alcoholism also becomes a disease of the spirit.

Anatomy of an Alcoholic

Some personality traits consistent in most alcoholics are anger, fear, guilt, shame, or entitlement issues. These traits usually come from the past or even the present. An alcoholic cannot control the alcohol, and this lack of control leads to lower self-esteem and feelings of failure in all aspects of life. Alcoholics don't believe they ever measure up or fit in, and many will overcompensate with words or actions to overcome their shortcomings. Within a short period of time, the alcohol is in control, but the alcoholic will never admit this. A lack of morals, values, and beliefs as well as a lack of humility or thankfulness are some of the causes of alcoholism. On the other hand, alcohol destroys morals, values, and beliefs. It knows no age or gender, and no one is exempt. It disrupts the circle of life and changes one's path in life.

There is nothing good about cancer, but alcohol is different; it always starts out feeling like a good thing. Social drinking—champagne at weddings and cocktails at parties, for example—starts out feeling good. Unlike cancer, which never starts out good, alcohol starts out feeling so innocent and subtle, creating the illusion of happiness, good feelings, and cheer. Then it becomes a cancer and subtly takes the alcoholic's life, just as cancer does.

How do you know whether alcohol is a problem for you? If it causes you problems mentally, physically, socially, financially, or with your relationship, then alcohol is the problem. How do you know whether you are an alcoholic? You will know when you admit the fact to yourself and say, "I am an alcoholic." At that time, and only at that time, will you know and understand that you are an alcoholic. Only then can you experience the miracle of recovery. Or you can go on to drink until your death. These are the only two choices. You cannot fix what you won't admit.

Prepare yourself for an uplifting, spiritual awakening. All this book requires is a desire to stop drinking and a willingness to open your mind a little to some new learning. This is the only requirement to stop drinking. Become teachable and be part of the solution, not part of the problem.

Sometimes things we don't understand rule our lives. We go about our day-to-day living through habit and instinct, functioning by what we learned in the past—by our upbringing, education, and genetics, generally living by what works for us. Beliefs, morals, values, and goals guide some people. Some activities are routine; daily, we probably get up in the morning, eat two or three times during the day, and sometime later go to bed. The choices we make during that time rule our lives. *Choice* is a key word in changing behavior, habits, or one's way of thinking. It doesn't matter what the addiction or obsession is; the same basic rules apply in changing those choices or that behavior.

The information presented in this book doesn't specifically focus on one thing, but there is a sequence of actions one must take to lose the addiction. If we could stop our addiction in one easy action, we probably wouldn't have it. You started drinking one day, so you should be able to stop in one day, right? But this isn't how addiction works.

Alcoholics become alcoholics for many reasons. Negative aspects of character, sometimes called character defects, tend to take over and eclipse the positive traits that exist in all of us. In that sense, the alcoholic is a victim. But being a victim of life or biological circumstances doesn't offer an excuse to live in a negative and destructive world of our own making. Indeed, it's common for alcoholics to perceive themselves as victims due to external forces, but in reality they have victimized themselves.

Three Types of Drinking

- Binge drinking: These people drink a lot for a period and then stop. They may drink consistently for one week or two weeks every three months or every other weekend. When they drink, they consume a lot and then take days or weeks to dry out and regain their senses, and then they repeat the process. A binge may last days, weeks, or even months.

- Social drinking: Social drinkers consume alcohol at every social event. The social aspect makes it acceptable, except that as more and more alcohol is consumed at each event, these drinkers are likely to embarrass themselves or others at some point. Social drinkers will also make up more and more social events and excuses to drink, even justifying nonsocial events as social.

- Daily drinking: Daily drinkers are usually well maintained and controlled. Their drinking pattern has increased ever so slowly and has gradually increased over time, and their tolerance for alcohol is high. They don't need a reason to drink; they have already decided long before that it is part of their lifestyle; drinking just is. They have a million reasons to drink in case they need one, but they usually aren't interested in giving reasons because they aren't concerned about what other people think. These are usually referred to as "functioning alcoholics," who go to work every day and always find some way to drink, whether daily or consistently. They may refer to their drinking as medicine and are convinced it is good for them. The daily drinker's life centers around alcohol. Daily drinkers are convinced they are doing the right thing.

Victim Thinking

There is a concept called "victim thinking," which many alcoholics get into without realizing it. The more they drink, the less goes their way until soon nothing goes their way. This is an ever-winding-down spiral. Without realizing it, their thinking, vocabulary, attitude, and ability to bring good into people's lives deteriorate. Thus, they get into this victim thinking of how badly the world is treating them. They keep drinking, thinking they are normal and that this is a normal way of life.

How many people do you know who think drinking is normal? They used to see their drinking parents with friends, never realizing these friends were also drinking. But just as the parents' lives deteriorated, so will theirs. As less and less goes their way, the anger increases at about the same ratio. And then one day, they explode, just like a rubber band that keeps stretching until it breaks. Many explode internally, with numerous physical internal problems. Those who explode outwardly usually end up in jail or in newspaper headlines.

Life can get better if you're continually trying and are positive. But for the alcoholic, the downward spiral is so subtle that it isn't even noticeable. When people are rejected, they feel hurt; and after a while, they feel like victims. Once they have convinced themselves they are victims, the label or concept stays with them to the point that they don't know how to get out of it. Many alcoholics isolate themselves from everybody and everything, and they may always drink alone.

Alcoholics have this consistent feel-sorry-for-me attitude. It doesn't take long before someone forgets any and all positive ideas and thinking. This is a low bottom for an alcoholic, and some drastic action, rethinking, and relearning are needed to turn the person around. Victim thinkers are never at fault; what's wrong is always someone else's fault, or someone did it to them and made them what they are. Victim thinking is a good indicator of an alcohol problem. Alcohol is a depressant that perpetuates and magnifies victim thinking. Below are some questions that can help identify whether you have an alcohol problem.

Questions

Here are some questions drinkers can ask themselves:

- If alcohol doesn't do what it used to do for me, am I still drinking?
- If alcohol is so good for me, do I feel sick and sad all the time?
- If I drink alcohol, has alcohol hurt people in my life?
- If deep down I want to stop, am I still drinking?
- If I stop drinking, do I know how to live without alcohol?
- If I have a lot of problems, is alcohol causing them?
- If I have a million reasons to drink, do I have one reason to stop?
- If I feel old and tired, am I depressed all the time?
- If I feel good about myself before I drink, how do I feel during and after I drink?
- If I have financial, physical, or mental problems, is alcohol the cause?
- If I have problems with my stomach, heart, or blood pressure, can I admit that alcohol may be the cause? If I'm on medication, is alcohol the cause of this problem?
- If I admit that alcohol controls me, do I have a problem with it?
- If I have choices in my life, is alcohol my main choice?
- If I am drinking, do I usually drink alone?
- If I have tried to stop drinking, have I failed?
- If I am willing and have a desire to stop drinking, can I stop?

If you answer yes to a couple of these questions, you probably have a drinking problem. If your answer to the last question is no, either way seek out treatment, counseling, or an AA meeting because the only requirements to stop drinking are a willingness to learn something new and a desire to stop drinking. No one can help you until you help yourself. Whether you have a drinking problem or are an alcoholic, all that is required to stop drinking is a desire and a willingness.

Drinkers who already are in a fog usually won't deal with these types of questions; they are too confusing, and they may go against drinking. Alcoholics aren't honest enough with themselves in the first place; thus, there is the reason for being unable to answer. You can ask these questions to start bringing up the awareness level to the person drinking. Alcoholics get moments of clarity, and if you know when they are, that is the best time to start asking.

If you are the spouse or loved one of a person you may suspect is an alcoholic, you have a choice. Generally speaking, if you confront those you love and indicate they may have a drinking problem, you may very well expose yourself to confrontation and defiance. Yet the questions bear asking if you think you and the loved one with a problem can sit down and discuss the issue without fanning the flames of conflict. You can ask these questions to raise the awareness level of the probable alcoholic into some type of action.

Alcoholics sometimes have moments of clarity on their own. If you know when they are, these are the best times to start asking. Be kind, gentle, and understanding. Your loved one, who may have a drinking problem, didn't set out to be an alcoholic. Nobody does. The person suffers from a disease and needs compassion so change for the better through sobriety seems like a positive step to take. The answer for a nondrinking spouse is to be supportive of an alcoholic who is trying to change. Judging, criticizing, and constantly bringing up the topic doesn't work and will only bring out the defiance in the alcoholic and more drinking. The nondrinking spouse needs to be supportive, encouraging, suggestive, compassionate, and patient. Encourage seeking help through treatment, counseling, or an alcohol treatment center. This change or choice must come from within the alcoholic.

People who are addicted don't have a choice; they must have whatever it is they are addicted to. It is only when they lose the addiction that they, for the first time, have a choice to do it again. Most people get into addictions in ignorance, not knowing the consequences or what an addiction is. As in alcoholism, once the "ism" sets in, there are no more choices; they must have what addicts them, no matter what. Alcoholics will do and say anything to get more of their addiction.

When drinking stops, a change starts to take place. Many people inadvertently start making other changes unconsciously; when people start dealing with nutrition, for example, they will feel better. When that takes place, maybe they will try to dress better and take better care of their appearance; as more nutrition is practiced, they may start losing weight, a practice that will enhance their appearance even more. So with one change, you get four.

Lifestyle changes don't happen overnight, but one day the person will notice the change and realize he or she has changed. And the more and more the person practices the change, the more and more he or she will notice. Just from practicing good nutrition alone will come more energy, more and better thinking, a lightness in the body, a feel-good feeling, and a natural pride as the body either repairs or replenishes itself of lacking or missing vitamins and minerals. This good feeling will creep up on the person. As the person gets more energy, he or she will do more things; and if he or she is doing good things, more good things will happen. So with one basic change, many other things happen. To make change, take out of your life what isn't working and try new things. Those that work, keep; those that don't, eliminate.

Life is a lifelong learning process. It is the reason many people keep getting better and better. Once a person realizes this, he or she will continue to learn for his or her lifetime.

Addiction

If you've had an addiction for many years, it will take you some time to lose it. Once the addiction is eliminated, you will be aware of progress in as little as two days to two weeks. Don't dwell on this fact, but let me explain. Nothing you have tried in the past has worked to get rid of the addiction. The alternative to this program is to keep doing what you were doing, discard the program, and go back out and do it your way some more.

To eliminate an addiction, I use these words interchangeably: *addiction* and *obsession*. These words have a similar meaning. Obsession is something we do over and over again; we think about it constantly or do it on a regular basis, sometimes continuously. We may have been doing it for many years or decades.

Addiction usually refers to something we put into our bodies, such as food or alcohol; it's something we now need. Obsession usually refers to all the time one spends thinking about the addiction, and addiction is the actions one takes to fulfill it. So the two go hand in hand and can consume many waking hours, if not a whole life; thus, the phrase "You are obsessed with food." As in the case of alcohol, people who drink on a very regular basis are consumed with where the alcohol is stored. Where is tomorrow's supply? Is there extra for an emergency? How long will what I have last? Where is the money to get some more? This is the obsession. And this thinking goes on and on, day after day, and it never ceases because it is never let out of the mind. It doesn't take long before the body itself is physically addicted to alcohol, and now the body won't let the mind stop thinking about it. Addiction is about what you are using, and it is about why you are using it. The same general protocol used in this book can be applied to any other addiction including opioid addiction.

There are mental addictions or obsessions and physical addictions or obsessions; after a while, the two seem to become one with the use of alcohol. Don't argue about addictions or obsessions, because the purpose of this book is to show you how to lose the addiction, the never-ending craving, using a mental-step process and positive-living program.

You don't need to concern yourselves with why or how, only that this program works. You have to want the program; you need to be fed up with your lifestyle or your past. You need to have had enough of the addiction, and you must be tired of being sick and tired. I'll say it again: you must want sobriety more than life itself. A new day brings back the craving, but I will show you how to overcome it.

For everything you take out of your life, you need to replace it with something else. For example, if you spend ninety minutes per day eating and now spend thirty minutes, you need to find something positive to do for the other sixty minutes. If you do nothing, you will be thinking about what you used to do during the other sixty minutes; and if you continue to do nothing during that time, you will convince yourself to do the addiction again.

Recovery progress can be seen in as little as three days. Don't dwell on this fact but keep hope alive one day at a time. If you are a functioning alcoholic, nothing you have tried in the past has worked. What I am going to present to you is a program that works. Progress in recovery may be slow or may happen fast. Recovery is a step-by-step process, and how quickly you recover has a lot to do with your attitude. If you're positive and want to fix the problem, you'll make more progress than if you are negative or resistant about it.

Alcohol and illegal drugs are poisons people put in their bodies, and then they derive pleasure from them. But if you really think about it and you live it, the consequences soon become greater than the pleasures. The pleasure soon becomes a nightmare, and at some point, a line is crossed; this is called the "ism" in alcoholism.

"Too much of anything isn't good for a person." Have you ever heard that saying from your parents or teachers? It really is true, and the same holds true for alcohol. Alcoholics may want to stop drinking, but they don't really want to stop. Sometimes they go back and forth in their heads for a lifetime until the addiction kills them. They convince themselves that they really don't want to stop, and they get into this thinking every new day. Time and time again, people don't stop their addictions until it's too late. Too much damage has been done, too much insanity has set in, or they have done irreversible physical damage. Whatever your addiction is, it will cause you problems. We convince ourselves that whatever problems are being caused, something else is causing them, and the addiction will go away. Or we think we aren't really addicted; we are in control. It really doesn't work that way. The more you keep and hang on to the addiction, the more problems you will have. *Let go and surrender.* The more you try to stop drinking, the more you will fail. Surrender is the answer. Surrender to God's will for you and to the fact that you can no longer control alcohol.

Blackout

A blackout can be described as a brain state where so much alcohol is consumed (this varies by individual) that the brain becomes numb or anesthetized, and the body functions by instinct, but the brain is numb, malfunctioning, or semi-conscious. It's a place where many times there is no memory. This is the point where drinking drivers have an accident and don't remember it. They don't remember the accident—how they got there or what happened. The brain may not remember anything; even if they have hurt or killed someone, they sometimes don't remember. The point after semi-consciousness is being unconscious—passed out. A blackout is a state of non-mind or non-thinking; it's a trancelike state where the body is able to move around by instinct, but there is no reasoning; and with more alcohol, the person will slip into unconsciousness. Some alcoholics may describe this state as the "glow," in which everything in life and the world is good with a total peace of mind and where all problems disappear. Many alcoholics drink consistently for this glow.

Alcoholics who have blackouts while drinking usually excuse it as going to sleep and will never admit to a blackout, because they don't remember. They know something is missing, but they don't know what. They feel something isn't right, but they don't know why. Sometimes alcoholics will drive somewhere in a blackout and the next day not remember where they are or how they got there.

The blackout state is different in every person, because of the amount of alcohol the body can tolerate and process. Many people pass out at this point; this is a place where the body shuts down because it can no longer handle more alcohol. Genetics, mental chemistry, physical makeup, and tolerance will be different in each person.

If people take in too much alcohol too fast for the body to process, then alcohol poisoning can occur. Too much alcohol is consumed too fast and builds up in the mind, body, and bloodstream; alcohol poisoning can cause death. Young people who drink as fast as they can in contests are on a real fine line of death, and many times you hear of a person dying of alcohol poisoning, usually a young person. They haven't drunk enough over the years to build up tolerance, and their virgin systems can't process the alcohol fast enough. Death may occur instantly or soon after they have passed out. Drinking is like putting a poison in your system. When you put in a little, your body is able to process it out, but put in too much too quickly, and you shock the system. It might not be able to process the liquid toxin as fast as the person takes it in, and the body shuts down from the shock, possibly leading to death.

Alcohol by the Numbers

In the United States, 86 percent of adults use alcohol at some point or another, according to the National Institute on Health (NIH) and the National Institute on Alcohol Abuse and Alcoholism (NIAAA). There are an estimated 15 million adults with alcohol use disorder in this country today, and 1.3 million adults have received treatment at a specialized facility, according to NIAAA. A certain percentage of that 15 million would be considered alcoholics and people with a drinking problem who didn't receive treatment. In 2010, it is estimated that over two million people have recovered in the Alcoholics Anonymous program, and AA is a worldwide fellowship established in more than 180 countries, according to the Alcoholics Anonymous General Services Office in New York. Also note that there are 88,000 annual deaths from alcohol-related causes, and 9,967 annual deaths from alcohol-impaired driving. It's also worthy to note that 10 percent of US children live with a parent who has alcohol problems, according to NIAAA. According to NIAAA, alcohol is the fourth-leading preventable cause of death in the United States.

No alcoholic will tell you or admit they have a problem, until the problems are destroying them, until they admit defeat in life. On any given day of the week, or at any party or bar on a Saturday night, no one drinking will admit he or she has a problem with alcohol. This is the subtle secret of addiction; it isn't a problem and will never be a problem until the person admits that it is. Others around you may say you have a problem, and they may say it for years and years, but until you say to yourself, "Alcohol is causing me problems," no healing process can begin. If alcohol is causing you problems, then alcohol *is* the problem but only when you admit it.

Of the percentage of people who admit themselves to an alcohol treatment facility or program, or seek help of some kind, most will come out clean and sober. A treatment facility will start alcoholics off clean and sober with new learning, tools to use, and a lifestyle change, but to maintain that nondrinking lifestyle, they must continue to practice and learn a nondrinking lifestyle. Many go back to their old ways—old friends, old environment, and same old lifestyle—and start drinking again. They must really want to stop drinking and practice a new nondrinking lifestyle until it becomes a habit. Some will start drinking again and may go on to die from alcohol-related diseases, including insanity, financial destruction, and psychological or physiological destruction. It is the baffling mystery of addiction and why so little has been known on how to cure an alcoholic.

Many alcoholics never make it to a treatment facility or alcohol program. In 2010, there were 1.3 million people who sought out treatment, and there were 13.7 million people with a drinking problem who didn't seek treatment. That equates to 13.7 million people who may need help. Not included in these numbers are people who sought out help through Alcoholics Anonymous, one of the most successful programs I have seen. Because AA is an anonymous organization, their numbers aren't included in the official numbers.

There are those alcoholics who have used a treatment program or an alcohol program and relapse time and time again. Those who relapse consistently have a medical term called "Chronic Brain Relapse Syndrome." These people are incapable of being honest with themselves or others, and they refuse to learn a nondrinking program; they usually go on to die from alcohol-related diseases. This is the baffling mystery of alcohol addiction. The treatment for these people is long-term treatment, nine months or more to reteach them how to live.

I believe alcohol is a major destroyer of lives and families in this nation, but little is still known about the disease of alcoholism. Some physicians or psychiatrists understand it, and even fewer know how to treat it. Alcoholism is a combination of some chemical deficiencies in the brain and some learned or genetic behavior. It is a learned behavior that is passed down from generation to generation until the cycle is broken. Children watch their parents drink, and they see when, where, and why they do so. When a similar situation arises for them when they are older, they turn to alcohol, just as their parents did. This fact is evident from generation to generation.

Alcohol is involved in drunk driving accidents with and without fatalities. It is involved a majority of the time in marital problems, spousal abuse, and divorce. The majority of the time, it relates to the homeless and is involved in about 20 percent of the workforce, based on my experience working with large agencies. Alcohol, a sociological phenomenon, is legal, acceptable, and universal in this country and worldwide.

Here is the paradox; alcoholics are never cured, and they must practice a lifestyle, a program, a protocol free of alcohol for the rest of their lives. If alcohol is started again in a week, a year, or even twenty years later, the destruction begins again, right where it left off when the last drink was taken. The alcoholic must want to be free of alcohol. Alcoholics are broken people spiritually, mentally, and physically. Given the right tools, they can fix themselves, reinvent themselves, and go on to live happy, joyous, and free lives. They can become productive members of society.

Chapter 2

Alcoholism Prevention

Question: Can you prevent alcoholism? Answer: Yes. Don't pick up the first drink. Sounds too simple, maybe even ridiculous? If you are a young person or a long-term, hardcore alcoholic, the answer is the same. It truly is the right answer. People who are addicted don't have a choice. They must have whatever it is they are addicted to and will often do anything to get it. It's only when they resolve the addiction that they, for the first time, have a choice of whether to become addicted again.

Most people get into addictions in ignorance, not knowing the consequences or what an addiction is. Alcoholism prevention is about tools you must use in preventing alcoholism. All subtitles in this book are tools to be used for treatment, recovery, or maintenance. The simplest tool may be "Don't pick up the first drink." If you are someone who cannot consume only one drink, then this is one of the best tools for you. Prevention is about a lifestyle and what tools you have available to you. It is how you think: your actions, truthfulness with yourself, your morals, values, and beliefs.

Drinking usually starts out as a social behavior, whether people watched other people or their parents drink or they get into a social situation where everyone else is doing it, and they try it. Many people can stop, but some cannot. As the drinking continues, the progression is very subtle, and every once in a while, a little more is required for the person to get that same good feeling. No alcoholic ever starts out thinking, *I will have one drink, and then I'll be an alcoholic.* The norm is quite the opposite. *I can have one drink, or I can have ten. I am still in control of myself.* Alcoholics will claim to the last day of their drinking that they are in control of themselves, no matter how much they drink. It is only when they admit to themselves for the first time that they aren't in control that things can get better and a change can begin to take place.

Alcoholics usually try many times to stop drinking, but a tremendous fear sets in every time they get it in their head that they want to stop. Alcohol is a mental and physical dependency. True alcoholics don't know how to function without alcohol. Whatever pattern they have set they will follow time and time again, with one exception; the drinking time and the amount will subtly increase; this is a guaranteed fact of every alcoholic for this progressive disease. Recovery is also progressive. Alcoholics usually give up trying to stop drinking within a short period after they have stopped drinking. They just give up, and the addiction takes over again; their minds and bodies tell them they need another drink. Withdrawal symptoms will create fear, and this fear initiates excuses to drink. This pattern may repeat itself time and time again. One key factor is that alcoholics haven't replaced their drinking time with something else, something positive; they usually just try to stop drinking. It is imperative that alcoholics practice new learning and use a positive living program in their lives. This is the most important factor for an alcoholic in recovery or treatment—first, one second at a time, then one minute at a time, then one hour, and then one day at a time. It is imperative at this moment that an alcoholic replace the first hours and days with a positive activity or new learning.

Alcoholism can be prevented, and this book will give you some nutritional and vitamin combinations and some thinking and living protocols that will help prevent alcoholism and/or the cravings. It is more than just a vitamin that will prevent the "ism"; it is a lifestyle, a way of life, and a pattern of thinking that won't allow the alcoholism to set in. With the use of nutrition, vitamins and supplements, a person has now taken on the thinking of doing good things to himself or herself. Vitamins are an enhancement to health, and when people take it on themselves to prevent sickness and disease, they are highly unlikely to drink alcohol to excess. This is a mind-set that leads to wellness, unlike sickness. Nutrition and vitamins will help reduce the cravings. One theory in alcoholism is that there is a legitimate chemical imbalance in the brain, and that causes cravings. With the use of nutrition and vitamin supplements, that imbalance can be corrected, reduced, or eliminated; thus, the cravings are reduced or eliminated. See chapter 3 on "Health and Healing through Nutrition, Vitamins, Minerals, and Herbs."

Alcohol is the cause of many human catastrophes and many, many problems. If alcohol is causing you problems, then alcohol *is* the problem, no matter how subtle.

Alcohol in any form is a toxin. If you can, focus your mind down, picture a cell in a microscope, and add alcohol; the cell shrivels and dies. Now take a billion cells, such as a human body and add a little alcohol; some cells die. Over years and years of drinking, whenever alcohol is added and more cells die, after a point in time, you may have full-blown failure of organs, minds, hearts, stomachs, livers, and so on. With each drink of alcohol, only a little is destroyed at a time, and then years later, when physical problems start and you get a moment of clarity in life, you realize alcohol has caused this to you. Did alcohol cause this to you? Or did you cause this to yourself? It is your arm that places the glass to your lips.

Here is a paradox. Does alcohol cause the addiction? Or does the personality cause it? In our world today, there are medical doctors and hundreds of studies on alcohol, opinions, books, and treatment centers just for alcohol addiction. All are still trying to answer that question. The answer is probably both. It is a learned behavior with a chemical imbalance in the brain. Alcohol isn't a problem until somebody drinks it.

One primary factor is that the personality causes the addiction. For an addictive personality, alcohol isn't a problem until one picks up the glass. Alcohol is one of a few deliberate diseases. In no other disease does the victim deliberately give himself or herself a disease. No one *tries* to get cancer, a stroke, or Alzheimer's disease. But with alcohol, a person may deliberately and unknowingly give himself or herself a variety of diseases. As with alcohol, a person can deliberately destroy himself or herself. This is why I refer to it as a subtle disease. First, it is the pleasure, and then it is the pain. After time there is no more pleasure associated with alcohol, and this fact is seldom learned from generation to generation, from parent to child. This scenario is repeated time and time again: family to family, dad to son, and grandparent to grandchild. Any one person can break the cycle.

Alcohol destruction begins with the finances, then maybe with the relationship, and then maybe with cirrhosis of the liver, a stroke, cancer, or other alcohol-related diseases. Add in a lack of exercise, overeating, and the American diet which may be lacking in fruits and vegetables and high in fat and fast food. Add a little stress, and you're on your way to alcoholism. The key to the prevention of alcoholism comes down to maintaining a healthy lifestyle, mind, body, and spirit—and just don't pick up the first drink.

Use a higher power or God. Define a higher power: a person, place, thing, or God, as you understand him. People use this higher power to help them live day to day without the addiction and to overcome the cravings. Positive-living programs may use the positive power of the group. Everyone in the group helps, supports, and encourages each other to stop drinking. In this program, don't beat yourself up if you fail today. What is important is that you keep trying. Those in positive-living programs focus on positive things and not negative things anymore.

Get up each morning and pray to do good today, and at night pray again and be thankful for the good you did today. Whatever method you use, get a higher power—God, a support group, whatever works for you. Use that power to help you before you take that next drink. Use that power to help you stop the addiction. The first hours and days will be difficult, but within two weeks, a new line will be drawn that will make each day easier. No person can do it alone, and if you are a religious person, God will get you through it. Using God as the higher power when you are ready will give you a tremendous amount of strength religious people know and understand. Let your pride down long enough to help yourself, to free yourself from whatever controls you. You have the right to use whatever you need to stop the addiction. You are special enough that you have that right. Here is a saying: "If you don't bend your knees and pray, you will bend your elbow for another drink" (anonymous). Pray to God for help.

Seven Sins

There is a concept called the "seven sins." All addicted personalities seem to have one or more of these to an extreme. The seven sins are pride, greed, lust, envy, sloth, gluttony, and anger. Most people may have some degree of these sins. It is when you have an extreme amount in any one of them that you create an imbalance and related problems. Too much jealously or envy will get you into a lot of possessiveness and trouble with spouses or other people, always wanting what other people have; too much pride will let you talk like a big shot and won't allow you to change, because you are already perfect. Too much pride will give you a sense of entitlement, thinking you're special and that everyone owes you. Too much greed will lead to lying, thieving, and manipulating people out of money; and too much gluttony will allow you to never get enough of anything. Too much anger won't allow you to see things objectively and clearly; anger will control you. Too much lust will lead to self-centeredness and constantly seeking out sexual pleasures. Too much sloth will lead you to living disorganized and messy, with self-centeredness, closed-mindedness, and justification that everything you do is right. Being able to recognize whether you have an extreme in any of the seven sins can be a key to preventing alcoholism.

Perfectionism

Many alcoholics are perfectionists. Because their bodies and minds are subtly deteriorating at an accelerated pace, many overcompensate with perfectionism. Willful perfectionism is the opposite of spirituality. As more and more drinking occurs and the brain degenerates, everything must be done routinely in their minds since their minds are no longer flexible enough to handle a variation of that activity or thinking. They no longer have the capability to be flexible or more creative in their thinking or living; thus, the word *controlling*. Alcoholics are known to be controlling people, because their thinking has become so very narrow minded that they don't know how to handle any deviation of their perceived way that things should be done. An alcoholic's vocabulary decreases with each year of drinking; thus, with decreased vocabulary, the lower their ability to communicate or deal with life problems.

In the first days and weeks of sobriety, if alcoholics have finally set in their minds that the alcohol has to stop, there is first a total relaxation of the mind and body, because a toxin isn't being put into the body anymore. Since the alcohol tolerance level has increased over the years to handle more and more alcohol each year, suddenly the tolerance doesn't matter, because today there is no more alcohol, and the mind and body begin to heal. This can take a few days or months, depending on the damage done. As more sobriety sets in, so will more flexibility in dealing with life problems. Recognizing the characteristic of perfectionism is a key in preventing alcoholism.

Religion and Spirituality

Spirituality is one of the five areas of life, and not enough can be said about spending time in this area. Spirituality is a main tool in alcoholism prevention, recovery, and long-term maintenance. This may be one of your greatest and hardest searches, but the reward will be great. It will give you that peace of mind you have been seeking in terms of validating yourself, being at peace with life and death, and continuing to do good things in your life. Once you learn to let go of the past, give your problems to God, and seek inner peace, you will now be able to do good things.

Any person troubled by divorce, death, or any other life-changing event cannot progress to good things until the event has been dealt with. Let go of it, give it to God, and you are ready to move on in your life. A person can hold on to the death of a loved one, anger, revenge, guilt, or shame forever. Or the person can let go of it today and start his or her life again.

Holding on to the past will control you, your thoughts, and your actions. It does take some courage, some deep inner decisions, and a desire to make your life better, progressive, and peaceful again. God is a savior, and if you can give your will and life over to the care of a God or higher power as you understand God, miracles will start happening. Don't ask how or why; they just will. Acceptance is the answer to all your problems.

Spirituality can take many forms, but prayer and meditation are the simplest and most private methods of seeking spirituality. Prayer is the simplest form through asking or seeking God's help, grace, or wisdom. I have sometimes heard meditation described as prayer. See "meditation" in chapter 4. Both prayer and meditation are tools to be used in alcohol prevention.

Here is a definition of church and religion compared to a spiritual program. Church and religion are belief systems, whereas some positive-living programs are spiritual programs. Alcoholics seem to relate better to a spiritual program, which is about a relationship with a higher power, compared to church, where they sit down, and the pastor tells them what the Bible says or what something in the Bible means. They are passive listeners. In a spiritual program, alcoholics take a more active role with their higher power. They actively work with a higher power in many areas of their lives, compared to taking a passive role in church, taking what was told to them, and trying to put that into practice. In the spiritual program, the person actively works with a higher power in praying, learning, and sharing life experiences to try to change certain aspects of his or her life, including cravings.

Working with the higher power is like working with someone, actively engaged in making changes with the help of that higher power. Spiritually bankrupt alcoholics may find it easier to accept a higher power than God. God seems to have some sociological definition that is too much for drinking people, or maybe they have had negative experiences with God, maybe as a punishing God who punished them in the past or when they were younger. Alcoholics now take a more active role in defining their higher power or God. This seems to make all the difference in the world to alcoholics, who now need a positive higher power or God to stop drinking.

Church, religion, or spirituality are a positive activity that will keep the mind occupied for a lifetime. They will teach good things in the process and give alcoholics a power greater than themselves. Many recovering alcoholics now find that church or spiritual activities bring a peace of mind they have never experienced in their lifetime. Many alcoholics find it hard to deal with peace of mind, since they have spent their drinking careers thinking grandeur thoughts and fantasies. This was one of the main reasons for the alcohol, the ability to be whatever they were lacking. Shop around for the church or spiritual activity you like. Pick your activity carefully and make sure their philosophy and goals are good for you. Church, religion, or spirituality all work in the prevention, treatment, and long-term maintenance of alcoholism.

If you ever notice, alcoholics socialize with other alcoholics, because they are their own group. No one else wants to be part of that group except another alcoholic. Recovering alcoholics are another group, and you sure won't find them socializing with drinking people. If you do, more than likely, they will also be drinking soon. Many recovering alcoholics don't understand in the beginning why they must stop socializing with their drinking friends. I have seen this problem time and time again, especially with younger people who are trying to fit in and are attempting to be a part of a group, and maybe a little fearful of being alone in life. They will stop drinking but continue to socialize with the same friends. They realize very quickly that they don't fit in. So they either join the drinking group again and do what they do, or the group puts them out because they don't do what the group does.

Alcoholics generally don't know how to function outside their group. This is also true for the alcoholic family, children of alcoholics, and alcoholics themselves; they don't know how to function in normal groups. This is why you see alcoholic families socializing with other alcoholic families or the nondrinking adult child of an alcoholic who marries an alcoholic. People will seek out what they know or groups of those who are like them. In life, stick with winners, people who are positive, progressive, and humble; people doing good things; people with good morals, values, and beliefs.

Spirituality or religion is a key tool in preventing alcoholism. Having a God or a higher power, a church, or a positive-living program plays a key role in alcoholism recovery, treatment, and long-term maintenance of the disease of alcoholism.

Sometimes the best prevention is education and knowledge. But once the addiction sets in, all the knowledge and education in the world are thrown out the window. Why? Because we are human and fallible. Because we aren't perfect. This is the baffling malady of alcoholism. Sometimes no matter how much education and knowledge we have, the best answer is still "Don't pick up the first drink."

Not-so-smart people don't learn from their mistakes. Smart people learn from their mistakes. Wise people learn from other people's mistakes.

—Anonymous

Chapter 3

Alcoholism Treatment—Health and Healing through Nutrition, Vitamins, Minerals, and Herbs

When treating alcoholism, consult a physician or treatment center. Withdrawal from alcohol can have serious mental or physical consequences, including death. Treatment in this chapter has a broad general meaning and can mean getting treatment in an alcohol treatment center, working a positive-living program, going to church, getting counseling, or trying nutrition and exercise. Treatment is a broad concept and encompasses many different processes in dealing with alcoholism. Withdrawal from alcohol should be done only under the supervision of a physician, starting with the first phase of withdrawal from alcohol to the second phase of the initial treatment of healing the mind and then the third phase of healing the body. This chapter covers all three phases.

Treatment consists of healing the mind, the body, and the spirit. Healing the mind is done with nutrition, taking vitamin supplements, eliminating alcohol from the brain, learning a new and different way to live, implementing some new tools, and working a positive-living program that will teach you a new way to live without alcohol.

Healing the body is done with nutrition, supplements, and exercise. Treating or healing the mind is foremost, because once the mind begins healing, the body will follow.

Healing the spirit is done with new and different teachings, a new and different way to live and think. A positive-living program such as Alcoholics

Anonymous or a church will teach people to incorporate God or a higher power into their thinking and lifestyle. It's in this area that new tools will be learned as a new way to live. Healing the spirit is an internal choice an individual makes. Accept the grace of God without question, and miracles will follow. By accepting grace, you will receive hope, and by receiving hope, you will gain faith.

Physically alcohol affects the liver and kidney, the brain, the stomach, the digestive system, the central nervous system, and the heart. It affects every cell in the body. It affects the mind, the thinking, and the actions. It destroys the most essential vitamins and minerals in the body, where many of these are needed to interact with each other to support life. There are whole-life functions, life cycles that need vitamins; they are a whole circle of life. Alcohol interrupts these life processes, and then there are numerous ailments, diseases, and alcohol-related problems. It is a toxin; it isn't a natural food. When you add a toxin to your body on a consistent basis, there will be negative results. When you do the actions, you also do the consequences. As better nutrition, vitamins, and minerals are supplemented, the cravings for alcohol will decrease.

Alcohol can deplete the body of needed vitamins and minerals to deathly deficient levels. As the body and mind begin to heal, there first sets in a feeling of helplessness, of not knowing what to do now. The mind and body keep telling each other something is missing; alcohol that has been needed for years is now missing, and desperation sets in, along with confusion, fear, and a feeling of dying. It is this feeling and fear that will start an alcoholic drinking within a few days after stopping. These confused feelings of fear are the closest thing an alcoholic will encounter to a near-death experience, which it is. Some alcoholics actually die at this point in time, because the mind and body are so out of balance nutritionally and chemically that they cannot get back in balance quickly enough to maintain life. Many physicians and professionals recommend hospitalization or admittance into an alcohol treatment center to withdraw from alcohol because of the life-threatening consequences of withdrawal and the initial treatment before and after withdrawal. After years of drinking, there are specific vitamins that are significantly depleted, and when the body needs these to support life, they aren't there to be used.

Nutrition and vitamin supplements are key to recovery for alcoholism. See below for a suggested protocol of nutrition and vitamins and minerals to be used in the recovery of alcoholism to help bring a person back into health.

The treatment to repair all the damage alcohol did over years of use is rather complex, compared to the prevention of alcoholism, which is relatively simple. Many times people are beyond repair in their thinking, and they just continue to drink to death. Only a true alcoholic really understands the internal and mental devastation alcohol causes for that short high period compared to the sickness and nausea that make up that period after too much alcohol is consumed or the next day, referred to as a hangover. On the short term, only one thing makes it go away for the alcoholic: more alcohol.

If alcoholics could see beyond today, they would truly change their lifestyle. With the right knowledge, long-term alcoholics can feel one hundred times better than their best drinking day in as little as two or three days. It is the rest of the work, of developing a nondrinking lifestyle, that takes longer. The saying goes like this: "For everything you take out of your life, you must replace it with something." If an alcoholic was spending five hours a night drinking, he or she must now find something else to do for that five hours. A hard task, yes. The person must put something constructive and positive into those five hours.

Initially, when alcohol is stopped, alcoholics may appear to be totally confused. Actually their brains may be in a state of shock, almost like the influence of an anesthetic; they are usually mentally paralyzed, in a fog, or everything is unclear. That's why the first few days of nondrinking are crucial to recovery. In a few days, alcoholics left on their own accord are likely to become mentally active, feel better, and drink again. The success to recovery—the alcoholic must desire to stop drinking, and as the alcohol is taken away, new learning must begin. Until the alcoholic desires not to drink, rather than to drink, no recovery can be made. Sometimes, two weeks later, months later, or years later, the alcoholic may make a choice to drink again. Every day the alcoholic must wake up and desire not to drink, more than he or she desires to drink.

If one day a recovering alcoholic wakes up with the desire to drink, he or she must have tools to combat that thinking; these include knowledge and nutritional information available to help them lose those cravings. Other tools include a thinking pattern that will overcome the desire, the mental power to say no to themselves, and the ability to substitute good actions to their thinking. If and when alcoholics do this, they will be recovering alcoholics, a success to themselves, their families, everyone around them, and everyone they will come in contact with. For now, they are children of goodness, of God. This is the miracle.

No one forces alcoholics to put the glass to their lips. The success of stopping alcohol consumption rests in the individuals' desire to quit, their desire to do good things to themselves. Alcoholics must want to quit. It's easy to walk around and be the victim of many things, but it's a lot harder to take responsibility for all areas of your life. Take responsibility; your life depends on it.

Instincts

When alcoholics drink, they function in a lowered state of awareness but a heightened state of instincts. This will be important to know later in sobriety, as recovering alcoholics literally have a sixth sense. During drinking, this heightened state of instincts is what leads to bar room brawls, fights, arguments, anger, or a fearful nature or perception that something or someone is out to get them. If you verbally insult drunks or make threats against their self-esteem or pride, they will retaliate negatively, either verbally or physically.

In the first days of sobriety, the environment must be quiet, because of a heightened sense of hearing, feeling, touching—all the normal senses. It's highly likely that there will be symptoms of withdrawal, such as hallucinations, shaking, confusion, profuse sweating, and DTs (delirium tremens) during this period, which can usually last one to five days.

If an alcoholic can get to day three and then day five, some sense of reality starts to set in. Although the body will want to reject good, nutritious food, the mind still craves the habit and the numbing effect alcohol has on the mind. This creates the confusion; the body no longer recognizes what is good and bad for it. The alcoholic has been putting something bad in it for years or decades, and now, in a few days, it wants more of the bad—the habit, the need, the craving, the glow, the addiction.

Alcoholics have minds that have been instinctively fine-tuned. They can justify anything they want without regard to morals, values, or beliefs. They have spent so much time being untruthful with themselves, always going beyond acceptable limits and boundaries, always trying to be something they are not, that some of this behavior manifests itself during social occasions, with spouses, or in bars. This can occur anywhere and anytime, and other people may perceive this as somewhat twisted thinking, which may be very subtle, or it may be blatant and loud or even physical.

I refer to the person addicted to indulgence, who continually seeks pleasure in one form or another, as pleasure seekers in life. Love isn't putting things in your mouth; it isn't sex, and love isn't found in a needle or a bottle. Love isn't hurting yourself. Love is doing good things for yourself and others, caring for others, and showing compassion, understanding, and patience. Love is having morals, values, and beliefs; it is liking yourself. There is an old common saying that love shouldn't hurt. Love shouldn't make you drunk, and love shouldn't cause you problems.

No alcoholic gets sober without help, whether that help comes from a higher power, friend, program, physician, treatment center, psychologist, or spouse; every person who stops the addiction needs help.

Treatment and recovery go hand in hand. Most of the subtitles in this book are tools to be used in treatment and recovery. Treatment consists of monitoring and healing the body during the first few days after alcohol is stopped. Getting the right nutrition and supplements is instrumental in healing the body and getting through the withdrawal process.

For some people, the more they drink, the more they want; it becomes a vicious circle or what's known as a double-edged sword. Alcoholics drink to lose depression, and the more they drink, the more depressed they become. The more depressed they become, the more they drink. The same is true for the physical nature of alcohol. If one is deficient in certain vitamins or minerals to begin with, the person may experience cravings; then he or she drinks alcohol instead of getting nutrition, and alcohol accelerates the deficiency and causes the loss of many vitamins and minerals in the body. If a person experiences nutritional cravings and substitutes alcohol, then the next day he or she experiences more nutritional cravings. This is the double-edged sword again.

Alcohol affects every cell in the body, and the damage may not be seen for many years. Alcohol is broken down in the liver, and drinking alcohol inhibits the liver's ability to absorb vitamins A, D, E, proteins, and fats. Vitamins B and C aren't retained by the body and are eliminated daily, but now with drinking, the body cannot absorb or retain them. The deficiency and damage start with alcohol consumption.

Cirrhosis of the liver is progressive and can be a final and deadly consequence of alcohol. Alcohol gradually and subtly destroys the liver in many people until inflammation, hardening, and scarring take place; then the liver can no longer filter toxins in the body, and the toxins begin to build up in the body. During actual liver or kidney failure, toxins and urine are stored just under the skin, and legs, arms, or a whole body may have a swollen appearance. Liver failure is one of the final consequences of alcohol. The liver has worked overtime for so many years due to drinking that its normal life expectancy is shortened. If taken care of with nutrition, vitamins, and minerals, the liver will last for decades. The liver is the only organ in the body that can regenerate itself. It can regenerate 25 percent or more of itself, but at some point with alcohol, if too much damage occurs, the liver cannot repair itself because it becomes too severely damaged.

One of the first physical consequences of drinking is damage to the nervous system, with loss of sensation to the hands, feet, or face; difficulty walking; or the beginning of diabetes. Problems also start with cholesterol, high blood pressure, heart palpitations, extra or skipping heartbeats, or an enlarged heart due to the fact that the heart must work harder and harder.

During the first three weeks after stopping alcohol, alcoholics will experience withdrawal to some degree. Common symptoms include hallucinations in vision or hearing, insomnia, convulsions, delirium tremens, rapid heartbeat, heavy sweating, night sweats, sudden anxiety attacks, confusion, some form of mental paralysis, and exhaustion.

Nutrition with vitamin and mineral supplements is essential for bringing the alcoholic back into health, and I don't want to understate their importance; they are essential for health for the recovering alcoholic. All vitamins are needed. Most can be obtained in a good daily multivitamin and mineral complex, but for the alcoholic, certain supplements are needed in the beginning of treatment. I have listed below those that are essential or important.

Once an alcoholic stops drinking and maintains good nutrition with vitamin and mineral intake, the insatiable alcohol cravings start to decrease. Nutrition is key to the prevention of alcoholism and to the maintenance of an alcohol-free lifestyle.

If you understand food and nutrition you know some people are already deficient in certain vitamins and minerals, and they will be susceptible to cravings. There is an age when teens and young adults experiment with new things, and once alcohol is tasted, their deficiency in vitamins is accelerated.

For young people with limited awareness about nutrition, alcohol is now preferred over food, because it makes them feel better than food, and the process repeats itself over again until such time that the "ism" subtly sets in. A person who drinks consistently or daily for twenty years may appear to be seventy years old when he or she is only forty.

Every alcoholic, during his or her drinking time if it is regular and consistent, will do damage to his or her mind and body. As you read each vitamin or mineral, this is what is specifically depleted, and the effects on the mind and body are devastating. Also included are some recommended nutritional foods and vitamins and mineral supplements to regain health from the damage to oneself, according to Dr. Balch.[1] All the vitamins listed below are supplements in addition to nutrition, and the most important vitamin is a good daily multiple green vitamin and mineral, also known as "Green Source" or the "Green Vitamin."

Free Radicals

Here is the simple explanation of free radicals. Free radicals come from everywhere and occur naturally. They are produced as a by-product of normal cellular activity. They occur from psychological and physiological stress. Free radicals come from chemicals, pesticides, radiation, toxic waste, cigarettes, alcohol, coffee, and barbecued and fried foods. Free radicals cause both natural and accelerated aging. With the use of antioxidants, you can slow down aging and repair damage that has been done, as in the case of alcohol. Many of the vitamins, minerals, and herbs listed below are referred to as antioxidants. [2]

If you have damaged your health through the use of alcohol, the following nutrition, vitamins, minerals, and herbs are for you to take to bring your health back up to a healthy level. If you are a drinking person who is going to stop drinking alcohol today, the following list is for you.

Vitamins

Note: If you are taking prescription medications, always consult a physician before introducing vitamins. Some medications have an adverse interaction with certain vitamins. Consult your physician.

---

[1] Phyllis A. Balch and James F Balch, *Prescription for Nutritional Healing* (London: Penguin, 2010), 18–135, 170–177.
[2] Gary Null, *Gary Null's Ultimate Anti-Aging Program* (New York: Kensington, 1999), 9, 118–120, 157, 262, 273–274.

Serious nutritional deficiencies begin to develop with alcohol intake, which is the start of mental and physical problems. At the end of this chapter, there are some suggested specific examples and a recommended protocol for rebuilding the liver due to cirrhosis of the liver, one of the most common diseases of alcoholism. Recovery can be helped by nutrition and a daily diet generous in vitamin supplements. Alcoholics also need to be aware of extremes of eating sugary, salty, and fatty food; less is better.

Vitamin A is needed for proper functioning of the eyes, sight, and correction of poor vision, anemia, and faulty hearing. Vitamin A is depleted in a slow manner, and once it is depleted from the body, you will notice eye infections, night blindness, blurriness, dizziness, and spots. In the later extremes of alcoholism, you may notice hallucinations, a distorted transaction between the mind and the eyes. Lack of vitamin A will also cause dark circles under the eyes, bloodshot (irritated) eyes, puffiness, and a facial feeling of bloat around the eyes.

Night blindness is common in alcoholics, and driving becomes difficult. The difficulty isn't so much seeing lights but not seeing everything else that isn't as bright as a light. Alcoholics cannot focus on light because the pupil is dilated, and the light coming in appears more than it really is, causing an irritant effect on the brain. It also causes the drinker to look away from the light and squint. Drinking causes liver damage, which causes a depletion of vitamin A. Depletion of vitamin A also causes ulcers.

People in treatment may take vitamin A daily for three weeks and then start a regular supplement of one vitamin A tablet every few days or follow the label instructions. You can get vitamin A in dairy products, milk, butter, eggs, liver, yellow vegetables, carrots, turnips, spinach, and yellow squash. Juicing is the fastest way to absorb vitamin A. A deficiency in vitamin A can be determined by looking at the fingernails; unhealthy nails aren't a bright, distinctive pink color underneath. Your nails will be in a bad shape—not well formed and easy to break. Other signs of deficiency include frequent infections in the eyes, cloudy vision or night blindness, dry eyes, and brittle and frizzy hair. Dry, frizzy hair is a frequent symptom of alcoholics because of a deficiency of vitamin A. Vitamin A is a healing vitamin and a powerful protectorate of the eyes and hearing. This vitamin is essential.

Vitamin B consists of vitamin B-1 (thiamine), B-2 (riboflavin), B-3 (niacin), B-5 (pantothenic acid), B-6 (pyridoxine), and B-12 (methyl cobalamin). Vitamin B is the foundation of health. It is depleted rather quickly and very steadily with alcohol consumption. Lack of vitamin B will cause dysfunction in the brain. Vitamin B is necessary for the steady and smooth flow of brain waves and energy. When vitamin B becomes depleted through the use of alcohol, all areas of the body are affected. Symptoms include shaking, unsteady hands, inability to reason, and a slow decrease in thinking ability. Sentences are very short, lack thought, and slowly begin not to make sense.

A deficiency of vitamin B for alcoholics means the world starts to cave in on them while they slowly go from a balance between objective thinking to subjective thinking. When they are truly alcoholics, they no longer have any objective thinking left; everything becomes subjective and totally self-centered. They are totally consumed with getting more alcohol, including the money to buy it and where to consume it. Thinking becomes very erratic, with outbursts of emotion. Persons may talk to themselves and always try to rationalize some thoughts. Depending on one's personality, this is where you will see extreme cases of "big-shotism," paranoia, schizophrenia, dementia, Alzheimer's disease, short and long-term memory loss, and the inability to focus on such things such as counting change or money because of a deficiency in vitamin B.

On the first day an alcoholic stops drinking, consistent doses of vitamin B need to be supplemented as well as foods high in B vitamin, such as fish, eggs, meat, and green vegetables. Alcoholics may be in different stages of dehydration. In extreme cases of dehydration, for example, the brain is dangerously depleted of water. Alcoholics will drink more and more alcohol until they sleep or pass out, but the next morning they will be totally dehydrated because alcohol dehydrates the body. There is also the fact that when alcoholics are drinking, they don't usually drink water, and drinking alcohol with water is no substitute. So the next morning, massive amounts of cool water will be consumed to satisfy this now-incomprehensible craving for water. This usually comes after days and days of drinking. As an example, this trait may be evident in elderly people, who forget to drink water and lose the craving for it. Dementia can set in, and if the problem isn't corrected, permanent damage to the brain begins. The same is true for an alcoholic.

Alcoholics consistently look over their shoulders to see who is behind them or following them, who is watching them drink or watching them drink and drive; this results in paranoid behavior. This behavior can be maintained for long periods, even decades, before it gets worse and is noticeable to the outside person. Short and long-term memory loss occurs daily and isn't even noticeable to the alcoholic, who passes it off as old age—no big deal; it's normal. But the problem becomes noticeable to someone close to and around the alcoholic. Things no normal person would forget are forgotten, and the alcoholic may remember them much later. Because of this uneven and erratic thinking alcoholics now maintain, they constantly fight to maintain control, but always, very slowly and subtly, they lose control of different aspects of their minds and bodies.

Vitamin B deficiency is the main problem connected with chronic alcoholism, but every vitamin is needed to repair the physical and mental damage alcoholics have done to themselves. Different individuals have different needs for vitamins or different amounts of vitamins. A deficiency of vitamin B causes stress, emotional imbalance to the point of being mentally ill, lack of energy, and a lowered immune system, which is highly susceptible to colds or flu. Vitamin B is needed daily since alcohol will deplete the body of vitamin B and other vitamins. Nutrition and vitamin B also decrease the craving for alcohol and may play a key role in recovery. Once drinking is stopped and nutrition and vitamin B intake increases daily, this step may help decrease the craving and play a major role in the alcoholics' success in not drinking.

Alcohol causes a deficiency in vitamin B, which causes protein not to be absorbed in the proper manner. Thus, alcoholics cannot digest protein, and their bodies are unable to produce hormones, enzymes, and neurotransmitters vital to carrying messages from the brain to the body. A vitamin B deficiency is noticeable by stumbling, slurring words, falling down, and suffering loss of body control.

Alcohol also causes damage to the lining of the stomach so it cannot absorb nutrients properly. If one person is eating well and drinking alcohol, whatever vitamins are stored in the body are used solely for digestion instead of other needed functions. If a person is eating poorly, with a lot of processed and fast food that is high in sugar and salt, the digestive system and vitamin storage are affected even more until the vicious cycle is present again. Vitamin B complex is the most necessary and needed vitamin of all vitamins. Nutrition and vitamin B complex is used to regain health from alcoholism and is instrumental to avoid a relapse.

Vitamin B may be found in the following foods: all fish (especially salmon), liver, spinach, brown rice, whole grain breads or grain cereal, eggs, green vegetables, wheat germ, rice bran, peanut butter, oatmeal, milk, raw nuts, beans, seeds, fruits, vegetables, meat, poultry, soy foods, broccoli, brussels sprouts, raisins, cheese, mushrooms, molasses, peas, walnuts, sunflower seeds, carrots, bananas, cabbage, corn, potatoes, cantaloupe, clams, and kidney beans.

A deficiency in vitamin B can cause rash, mouth sores, fatigue, flabby muscle tone, a loss of appetite, depression, nervous disorders, premature graying, a lowered immune system susceptible to colds and flu, a coated or blue tongue, an enlarged liver, stomach problems associated with gastritis, and other diseases. Also, an enlarged heart, weight loss, weak muscles, breathing problems, nerve problems, heart problems, digestive problems, blurry vision or other eye problems, sensitivity to light, headaches, depression, insomnia, dizziness, trembling, mental fatigue, high cholesterol, diarrhea, mental imbalance, schizophrenia, dementia, malnutrition, hallucinations, arthritis, teeth grinding, convulsions, anemia, irritability, personality changes, memory loss, and rapid heartbeat.

A good B complex vitamin will contain all the Bs in one tablet. When one is losing the effects of alcoholism, the B vitamin with nutrition is the single-most important vitamin but not the cure-all for the disease. Reversing the effects of alcoholism and preventing drinking in the future require a full range of nutrition and vitamin supplements. Vitamin B is an essential supplement.

Vitamin C is best defined as the miracle vitamin. While vitamin B is essential to the alcoholic who stops drinking, vitamin C can within a few days make the alcoholic feel wonderful in mind and body. Vitamin C and balanced nutrition is just as important in controlling, preventing, and suppressing the alcohol addiction. Vitamin C works very quickly, within days, and will help an alcoholic lose the craving. Alcoholics are notorious for being meat-and-potato people, but most are generally lacking fruits and vegetables. Since vitamin C is lost out of the body daily, this deficiency may go on for a long period.

Alcoholics may have a minimum amount of vitamin C in their bodies at any given time, since vitamin C can come from many sources. There are two things that make an alcoholic feel well; one is vitamin C, and the other is natural sugar that comes from fruit juices or sugar. Vitamin C will give the new nondrinker a feeling of elation, a natural high, and a sense of well-being. On the day an alcoholic stops drinking, he or she should take vitamin C daily along with vitamin B. The daily intake may be adjusted after a few weeks when the body has had some time to heal itself. Follow the directions on the label.

Many alcoholics lose a tooth or part of a tooth; this loss is a mystery to them. The answer is that the lack of vitamin C leads to scurvy. Vitamin C was the miracle cure on ships that were sent out to sea for long periods of time. With a lack of vitamin C, the gums and teeth become weak and loose, and they may have other problems. I have talked with many alcoholics who asked me about why they are losing teeth or experiencing bleeding gums. These problems go along with the alcoholic characteristic that they usually don't eat enough fruits and vegetables or eat too small an amount or too infrequently, along with the alcohol that depletes vitamin C.

Vitamin C holds the cells together. Also note that all vitamins work together, so taking one and none of another still keeps the body out of balance; something is still missing. That's why it's most important for the alcoholic to take vitamin supplements in the beginning of treatment. This practice should and can last a lifetime, because a vitamin deficiency can lead back to the drink. Generally, after a few weeks of not drinking, an alcoholic's eating becomes better, and more and more vitamins are gained naturally with nutrition. An alcoholic who has drunk for twenty years needs consistency of nutrition with vitamin supplements to get his or her mind and body back to a healthy state.

As now-nondrinking alcoholics take nutrition and vitamin supplements, they will feel and know the difference in their bodies and their thinking, and they will feel better and better as more time goes by.

As an antioxidant, vitamin C is a major fighter of colds, flus, heart disease, and cancer. Vitamin C is daily at work everywhere and is especially efficient in preventing stress. Vitamin C will make a difference between wellness and sickness as well as how alcoholics live, look, feel, and age. Lack of vitamin C can endanger your life. A deficiency of vitamin C contributes to emotional disturbances, alcohol cravings, mental illness, drug cravings, schizophrenia, cancer, heart disease, blood diseases, bone and tooth disease, higher cholesterol, scurvy, large bruises or bleeding under the skin, bloodshot eyes, and infertility.

You can obtain vitamin C in oranges and all citrus fruits as well as in strawberries, cantaloupes, many vegetables, lettuce, broccoli, tomatoes, potatoes, brussels sprouts, cauliflower, cabbage, bell peppers, grapefruit, lemon juice, berries, green vegetables, asparagus, avocados, pineapples, spinach, peas, onions, radishes, turnip greens, collards, and bananas. The old wives' tale about eating oranges regularly or drinking a glass of orange juice in the morning is true. Vitamin C is essential.

Vitamin D is associated with bones and teeth. It is vital to bones and teeth, and the kidneys must have vitamin D to function correctly. Vitamin D also comes from the sun and helps the body use calcium.

A deficiency of vitamin D contributes to rickets, bone disease, osteoporosis, easy bone breakage, back pain, arthritis, rheumatism, brittle and fragile bones, pale skin, insomnia, and irregular heartbeat. You can get vitamin D from the sun, fish, tuna, salmon, sardines and herring, cod liver oil, dairy products, halibut, liver, oatmeal, sweet potatoes, and vegetable oils. Vitamin D is essential.

Vitamin E is known as the young vitamin, meaning it helps in the ability to reproduce. It is the vitamin most associated with wellness, antiaging, and skin tone and texture. It is also an antioxidant. Vitamin E provides strength and endurance. A deficiency of vitamin E contributes to mental illness, physical illness, advanced aging, heart disease, skin problems, infertility, cancer, diabetes, lack of energy, swelling in the face or legs, cramps, breathing problems, and cold fingers and toes. You can find vitamin E in oils, wheat germ, green vegetables, whole cereals and whole grain foods, eggs, nuts, vegetable oils, beans, seeds, brown rice, cornmeal, liver, oatmeal, soybeans, sweet potatoes, organ meats, and watercress. Refined and processed foods lose much of their vitamin E by sitting on a shelf. The best source of vitamin E is in supplement form. Vitamin E is essential.

When starting a program of recovery, nutrition and all vitamins listed above are essential for bringing the mind and body back into balance. Leaving one out may leave you out of balance and cause mental or physical problems in certain areas of your life. All vitamins are essential to maintain life.

Multivitamin and mineral complex offer the best source of a variety of all vitamins and minerals. A multivitamin may not be enough for a recovering alcoholic, who may need increased doses of certain vitamins and minerals once alcohol is stopped. Once the alcohol is stopped and the fog goes away anywhere from days to months, the brain and body become extremely aware that things aren't just right. It may take some time after alcohol is stopped for the person to regain some type of appetite because of the shock to the system of having no alcohol. Once alcohol is stopped, the body will begin to repair itself from years of being saturated with alcohol.

A multivitamin in the beginning is good but not enough. Consult a physician to determine what vitamins or minerals are extremely deficient in you. A good rule is to take one to three multivitamins daily, following the directions on the label. Take other essential and optional supplements according to directions on the label. The best multivitamin I have come across is known as a Green Source or Green Vitamin. Ask any reputable vitamin store for the Green Vitamin; it is a vegetarian vitamin, and the Green Vitamin is an exceptional multivitamin. It may have different names by different providers, but it is always known as the Green Vitamin. I recommend iron free, unless you have some medical need for iron or are a female still menstruating. A good quality multivitamin is essential and the most important supplement of all.

Here is a list of other essential and optional minerals, natural food supplements, and herbs that will bring the alcoholic back to health.

Minerals, Amino Acids, Antioxidants, or Natural Food Supplements

Note: If you are taking prescription medications, always consult a physician before introducing minerals, amino acids, antioxidants, or natural food supplements. Some medications have an adverse interaction with certain supplements in this category. Consult your physician.

Alpha lipoic acid aids in protecting the liver and pancreas from alcohol damage and is a powerful antioxidant. It is an optional supplement.

Amino acids are produced when protein is consumed. They are the building blocks of all proteins and can be obtained from meat, poultry, fish, beans, rice, nuts, corn, seeds, and wheat. This supplement is important.

Calcium is essential for strong bones and teeth and for a regular heartbeat and nerve impulses. Calcium lowers cholesterol and helps prevent heart disease. Its deficiency contributes to depression, delusions, convulsions, hyperactivity, thinking impairment, tooth decay, arthritis, heart palpitations, numbness, insomnia, cramps, high cholesterol, aching joints, and brittle nails. This mineral is essential.

Calcium can be obtained in dairy products, milk, seafood, salmon, sardines, green leafy vegetables, yogurt, watercress, soybeans, tofu, seeds, almonds, filberts, oats, prunes, figs, collards, goat milk, cheese, cabbage, broccoli, yeast, asparagus, and blackstrap molasses. This mineral is essential in a program of recovery. Calcium is an essential supplement.

Choline is part of the vitamin family and contributes to the transmission of nerve impulses and helps transmit the nerve messages from the brain to the spinal cord and throughout the whole nervous system. It also minimizes excess fat in the liver. Lack of choline contributes to brain and memory malfunction. Choline can be obtained in whole grain cereals, eggs, milk, meat, soybeans, and beans. This supplement is important.

Chromium is needed for energy and is involved in the metabolism of glucose. It is essential in the synthesis of cholesterol, proteins, and fats. This essential mineral stabilizes blood sugar levels. Deficiency in chromium may contribute to fatigue, anxiety, arteriosclerosis, and sugar intolerance. Too much chromium will cause kidney and liver ailments, ulcers, and skin problems. Follow the directions on the label.

Chromium can be found in whole grains, brown rice, brewer's yeast, meat, cheese, liver, chicken, dairy products, milk, eggs, potatoes, beans, and mushrooms. Don't take chromium if you are taking insulin; consult your physician. Chromium is an optional mineral.

Coenzyme Q10 is part of the vitamin family, a natural food supplement and antioxidant. It plays a critical role in the production of energy in every cell in the body. The role of CoQ10 resembles vitamin E. It is a powerful antioxidant that aids in circulation, stimulates the immune system, and increases tissue oxygenation. CoQ10 is most beneficial for cardiovascular disease, heart disease, high blood pressure, respiratory diseases, schizophrenia, Alzheimer's disease, obesity, tooth and gum disease, diabetes, and healing ulcers. The source of CoQ10 is salmon, mackerel, sardines, spinach, peanuts, and beef. CoQ10 is an important supplement.

Colostrum is the yellowish fluid secreted by the mammary gland of mothers in the first days after giving birth. It contains high levels of proteins and growth factors as well as immune factors. Colostrum can boost the immune system and accelerates the healing of injuries. Colostrum can only be obtained as a supplement, and it is an optional supplement.

Desiccated liver is concentrated dried liver that is put into a powdered or supplement form. It contains vitamins A, B complex, C, and D; it aids in liver disorders. This natural food supplement is optional.

Folic acid is considered a brain food and also strengthens the immune system. Folic acid can be obtained from asparagus, barley, beef, bran, brown rice, cheese, chicken, dates, green leafy vegetables, lamb, legumes, liver, milk, mushrooms, oranges, split peas, root vegetables, salmon, tuna, whole grains, and whole wheat. Folic acid is part of the vitamin family and is an important supplement.

Gamma-aminobutyric acid (GABA) is for brain metabolism and proper brain function. It acts as a neurotransmitter in the central nervous system. GABA can be taken to calm the body. It acts like a tranquilizer and prevents anxiety, hypertension, and stress without giving the fear of addiction. Too much GABA can cause anxiety, numbness, tingling, and shortness of breath. GABA can be used in the first weeks of stopping alcohol and thereafter, depending on the need. GABA is an important amino acid.

Glutathione is a powerful antioxidant produced in the liver. It is produced and stored in the liver, and it cleanses the liver. It detoxifies the liver, so you can see that after years of trying to rid the body of alcohol, the liver can use some help in the form of a supplement. If drinking has stopped, glutathione is essential to the alcoholic, and it will help detoxify the body and the liver of alcohol. Alcohol may reside in the body in some form or residue for three to four months after drinking is discontinued. Glutathione will also help put the liver back in shape. There are alcoholics with long-term drinking experience who have absolutely no liver damage at all; on the other hand, there are people with as little as a few years of drinking experience with some progressive damage due to cirrhosis of the liver.

A deficiency of glutathione may cause lack of coordination, tremors, loss of balance, mental disorders, and accelerated aging. Glutathione is a supplement and an essential antioxidant.

Inositol is part of the vitamin family and helps to reduce cholesterol and hardening of the arteries. It also aids to remove fats from the liver. Research has shown that it may help in the treatment of depression, obsessive-compulsive disorder, and anxiety disorders. Inositol can be found in fruits, beans, meats, milk, molasses, raisins, vegetables, and whole grains. This supplement is important.

Lecithin is essential to every living cell in the body. It is an emulsifying agent and helps prevent arteriosclerosis and cardiovascular disease. It improves brain function and aids in the absorption of thiamine by the liver and of vitamin A in the stomach. It promotes energy and is needed in the repair of the liver from alcoholism. Lecithin can be found in soybeans, eggs, fish, beans, grains, yeast, and wheat germ. Lecithin is an important natural food supplement.

L-Arginine enhances the immune system and is good for preventing liver disorders, cirrhosis, and fatty liver. It may be helpful in repairing damaged tissue. L-Arginine can be obtained in dairy products, meat, oats, peanuts, soybeans, walnuts, white flour, wheat, and wheat germ. This amino acid is important.

L-Carnitine is related to B vitamins. It helps to use fat as an energy source and prevents fat buildup around the heart and liver. The use of alcohol decreases fat metabolism and leads to an alcohol-related disorder called fatty liver. L-Carnitine enhances vitamins C and E. Deficiency in L-Carnitine can contribute to certain types of muscular dystrophy, obesity, loss of strength, diabetes, confusion, and heart pain. It can be found only in meats or cornmeal fortified with lysine. L-Carnitine is an optional amino acid.

L-Cysteine, a sulfur-containing amino acid that affects the skin, is important for detoxification. Cysteine detoxifies harmful toxins and protects the body, and it works best with vitamin E and selenium. It helps protect the liver and the brain from damage caused by alcohol and drugs. This supplement is essential.

L-Methionine is an amino acid and a powerful antioxidant that helps the digestive system and aids to detoxify harmful agents in the body. It helps prevent muscle weakness and prevents brittle hair. It helps mental illness such as schizophrenia, is a neutralizer of toxins in the liver, and helps protect it. L-Methionine can be found in foods such as fish, eggs, beans, garlic, onions, soybeans, seeds, yogurt, and meat. L-Methionine is an important supplement.

Lutein is part of the vitamin A family and helps prevent night blindness. Lutein reduces the risk of macular degeneration and cataracts. It can be found in a supplement form, and it is an optional supplement.

Lysine helps build muscle protein and tissue repair. It is also important for growth and bone development, and it maintains a proper nitrogen level and aids in the production of enzymes, hormones, and antibodies. Deficiency in lysine contributes to anemia, the inability to concentrate, irritability, lack of energy, bloodshot eyes, hair loss, poor appetite, weight loss, stunted growth, and reproductive disorders. Lysine can be found in dairy products, milk, cheese, soy products, meat, fish, yeast, lima beans, and potatoes. Lysine is considered an essential amino acid. The amino acid is very beneficial for recovering alcoholics and is an important supplement.

Magnesium is needed for energy production and helps to prevent depression, muscle weakness, dizziness, stress, irritability, nervousness, kidney stones, cardiovascular disease, certain forms of cancer, and osteoporosis. It may reduce cholesterol, insomnia, seizures, rapid heartbeat, hypertension, heart attack, fatigue, pain, and irritable bowel syndrome. Almost all alcoholics are magnesium deficient, which results in sodium excess, no matter how little sodium is taken. Most foods contain sodium naturally, and too much sodium may cause damage of the pancreas.

We can obtain magnesium from dairy products, seafood, fish, salmon, meat, fruits, apples, apricots, bananas, cantaloupes, figs, peaches, brown rice, beans, nuts, soybeans, lima beans, black-eyed peas, whole grains, garlic, green leafy vegetables, avocados, wheat, blackstrap molasses, and brewer's yeast. This mineral is essential.

Manganese is needed for a healthy immune system, healthy nerves, blood sugar regulation, bone growth, fat metabolism, the production of energy, and fluid in the joints. Drinking alcohol causes someone to lose large quantities of manganese. Alcohol raises blood sugar very rapidly, and with time it is the major cause of diabetes or blood sugar disorders. Manganese can improve this condition. A deficiency of manganese contributes to confusion, convulsions, hearing and eye problems, high cholesterol, heart problems, memory loss, hypertension, irritability, rapid pulse, tremors, and tooth grinding. Manganese can be found in whole grains, seeds, nuts, avocados, and seaweed. It also appears in eggs, beans, green leafy vegetables, pineapple, and blueberries. Manganese is an optional mineral.

Melatonin is a natural hormone the brain produces to aid in relaxation and sleep. Taking melatonin (1–3 mg) nightly will greatly aid the alcoholic in getting a good night's sleep. It may contribute to one of the most natural restful nights of sleep an alcoholic has had in years. Melatonin is an optional natural food supplement.

Niacin (B-3) is different from the other B vitamins in that the body can produce its own. The alcoholic, on the other hand, is more than likely to be deficient in all B vitamins. Niacin is essential to every cell in the body, especially to the alcoholic. It aids in the function of the nervous system and digestive system. If depleted, essential metabolic functions may stop functioning. Niacin transforms sugar and fat into energy. A deficiency in niacin may cause arthritis, high cholesterol, heart problems, and mental illness as well as skin disorders, diarrhea, abnormal function of the intestines and digestion, malnutrition, and death. Niacin may help to control alcohol cravings. You can obtain niacin in organ meats, liver, kidneys, tuna, salmon, dates, figs, prunes, beans, peas, green vegetables, wheat germ, and brewer's yeast. Niacin is an essential supplement.

Potassium is needed for the nervous system and a regular heartbeat, and it helps in muscle contractions. It helps to control water balance in the body and to prevent strokes. It maintains stable blood pressure and regulates nutrition to each cell. Deficiency of potassium may contribute to fluctuations of the heart, high cholesterol, insomnia, low blood pressure, fatigue, weakness, chills, thinking impairment, depression, nervousness, sugar intolerance, nausea, vomiting, constipation, diarrhea, excessive thirst, dry skin, and respiratory distress. Drinking alcohol contributes to the loss of large quantities of potassium. Potassium loss can also cause magnesium deficiency.

Potassium can be found in bananas, avocados, brewer's yeast, brown rice, dates, figs, nuts, garlic, fish, dairy products, fruit, beans, poultry, meat, whole grains, vegetables, potatoes, dried fruits, and raisins. Potassium is an essential mineral.

Primrose oil is a natural food supplement that helps to prevent hardening of the arteries, heart disease, and high blood pressure. It relieves inflammation and is beneficial for cirrhosis of the liver. Primrose oil is essential.

Raw liver extract is an abundant source of needed B vitamins that aid in the repair of the liver. Many of the same vitamins in raw liver extract can be found in the B complex vitamin (B-2, B-3, and B-12). This supplement is essential if you have liver damage.

Selenium is an antioxidant that protects the immune system and helps to produce antibodies and maintain a healthy liver and heart. It has also been found to protect the liver from cirrhosis of the liver. Selenium also helps prevent cancer, gives energy, and maintains cholesterol. Too much selenium causes arthritis, stomach disorders, irritability, yellow skin, brittle nails, hair loss, and liver and kidney problems.

Selenium can be found in seafood, tuna, salmon, meats, liver, chicken, grains, nuts, Brazil nuts, dairy products, brown rice, grains, wheat germ, vegetables, onions, garlic, yeast, and molasses. Selenium is an essential supplement.

SAMe is a derivative of the amino acid methionine and is an effective antidepressant. It promotes health of the liver. SAMe should not be taken by anyone with a bipolar disorder and a physician should be consulted before using this optional supplement.

Taurine is the building block of all amino acids; it promotes a healthy heart. Taurine has a protective effect on a dehydrated brain, and it may reduce symptoms of alcohol withdrawal. Taurine can be found in eggs, meat, fish, and milk. It is an essential supplement.

Zinc promotes a healthy immune system, healing, taste, and smell; and it protects the liver. Zinc is essential to prostate gland function and growth of the reproductive organs. A deficiency of zinc contributes to fatigue, hair loss, impaired night vision, memory loss, colds, flu, loss of taste and smell, high cholesterol, thin fingernails with white spots, acne, impotence, prostate problems, diabetes, and slow healing.

Zinc is found in whole grains, yeast, sunflower seeds, soybeans, seafood, sardines, oysters, fish, pumpkin seeds, eggs, lamb, beans, lima beans, liver, meats, poultry, mushrooms, yeast, and pecans. Zinc is an important antioxidant.

Note to alcoholics who have mixed any kind of soda with their drinks for many years: You may have a problem with blood sugar, and you may experience a very unstable blood sugar level when alcohol is discontinued. Many alcoholics will try to substitute soda by itself after stopping alcohol. At first this measure will cause extreme highs by the sugar alone. Drinking soda in the beginning is just a continuation of the habit when there was liquor in the glass. Chromium is extremely good to stabilize mood swings in the beginning after discontinuing alcohol. Many alcoholics will develop some type or form of diabetes; this should be checked with a physician as soon as possible.

Herbs

Note: If you are taking prescription medications, always consult a physician before introducing herbs. Some medications have an adverse interaction with certain herbs. Consult your physician.

Alfalfa, one of the most mineral-rich supplements there is, contains chlorophyll, calcium, magnesium, phosphorus, potassium, and all known vitamins A, B, C, D, and E. Alfalfa has a neutralizing effect on the stomach and intestines. It is good for liver disorders, high blood pressure, ulcers, gastritis, anemia, gum and teeth infections, cancer, hemorrhoids, and asthma. Alfalfa is a natural food supplement. It is exceptional for recovering alcoholics because it helps multiple ailments and all disorders too familiar to an alcoholic. Alfalfa is an optional herb.

Aloe vera aids in the healing of stomach disorders, ulcers, and colon disorders. It is known for treating skin disorders and comes in a supplement form. It is an optional herb.

Burdock root is a strong antioxidant when used with vitamin E. Burdock root is an herb that helps protect against cancer and cell mutation. It is an optional herb.

Chlorophyll is a detoxifier and a blood cleanser. It can also provide other sources of minerals and enzymes, especially when taken in the "green drink" formulas. Green drinks are a mixture of phytochemicals including chlorophyll, mineral, enzymes, and other important nutrients. Chlorophyll is sold separately and is an optional herb.

Ginkgo biloba may greatly increase oxygen in the brain. It may give the alcoholic a great sense of awareness. Alcoholics will naturally gain a very clear awareness by stopping the alcohol, and ginkgo may help that process. Ginkgo biloba is an optional herb.

Grapeseed extract is a powerful antioxidant for the protection of cells. Grapeseed extract comes from the seed of a wine grape and vegetables. It strengthens and repairs the cardiovascular system, and it also protects the liver from damage. This extract is an important herb.

Kyolic, aged garlic, is one of the most valuable foods known to man. Kyolic may lower blood pressure, prevent heart attacks, lower cholesterol, aid in digestion, and prevent strokes. Garlic is used for many diseases and illnesses. It stimulates the immune system and is a natural antibiotic.

Garlic comes in natural form or supplements, salt or oil. Kyolic is essential to a recovering alcoholic.

Milk thistle contributes to cleansing the liver. Once an alcoholic stops drinking, the liver has the capability, like no other organ in the body, to repair itself, but it needs help with the right vitamins and minerals. Milk thistle contributes to cleansing the liver of all toxic chemicals and will help detoxify the body. Milk thistle is an essential herb.

Silymarin is an antioxidant used to treat liver disease. It protects the liver from alcohol and promotes the growth of new liver cells. Silymarin is an important herb.

St. John's wort is an herb specifically used for depression and viral infections. It is optional to the alcoholic, although it may make a person feel better, which is essential to a recovering alcoholic. It maintains a certain lightness for the person. Depression is one of the main mental attitudes alcoholics are left with, which they probably had before they started drinking. They will keep depression for life unless they learn a more positive lifestyle and positive thinking. St John's wort helps in this process and is an optional supplement.[3]

What becomes apparent is that drinking alcohol distorts the whole balance of the vitamin and mineral makeup of each cell and organ, the nervous system, and the brain. It is so subtle that it isn't noticed; it isn't recognized, and over time, bit by bit and piece by piece, the body and the mind are degenerated. Alcohol is not only silent; it is subtle.

Many alcoholics have some degree or partial degeneration of the liver. See cirrhosis of the liver below. Some find that their body is no longer capable of removing ammonia from the body or only to a partial extent, and they are left with partial cirrhosis of the liver for the rest of their lives. The liver is the only organ that can regenerate or rebuild itself, if the right vitamins

---

[3] Phyllis A. Balch and James F Balch, *Prescription for Nutritional Healing* (London: Penguin, 2010), 18–135, 170–177.

and minerals are supplemented with nutrition. A physician will put them on a lifelong diet consisting of fruits and vegetables and supplements. There is only one mineral and one food I have found in my research that will eliminate ammonia from the body. The mineral is manganese, which has the capability of removing ammonia, but manganese shouldn't be taken in large doses. Follow the directions on the label. The foods that have the capability of removing ammonia are kidney beans, peas, and soybeans. These help detoxify ammonia. Also eat raw nuts, goat's milk or goat cheese, fresh vegetable juice or green drinks, green leafy vegetables, and primrose oil.

Alcoholics have a hard time focusing on anything while drinking, and afterward, when alcohol is stopped, they may still have some problems focusing. This condition will remain for weeks to months after alcohol consumption ceases. The problem can be helped with nutrition and many of the supplements listed above, especially melatonin, vitamin B, vitamin C, zinc, ginkgo biloba, magnesium, and ginger root. Alcoholics have had stomach problems since their first week of drinking. Ginger root contributes to soothing the stomach. As each vitamin helps a specific problem, the alcoholics' mind and body will come back into balance. The key to supplements is consistency.

In the first days of nondrinking, alcoholics may be totally disorientated. It isn't unusual for hallucinations or delirium tremens to occur, and they may be totally involved with themselves. It takes a period for the body to physically heal itself from the physical damage to organs such as heart, stomach, kidney, liver, blood system, nervous system, and the brain. Then there is the mental damage, patterns of thinking that don't work without alcohol, a psychological mental dependence, and all kinds of "stinking thinking" that needs to be corrected. The first few days will determine whether the alcoholic will drink again. In those days the change and stress of no alcohol may be too much stress for the mind and body, so alcoholics may drink again within a few days. If they can make it past the first week, success may follow for months and then years. This is the reason some alcoholics voluntarily admit themselves to an alcohol treatment facility for one week to three months. This way they have no choice to drink.

All the vitamins listed above are essential to health; some of the minerals and herbs are essential, and some are optional. Normally after a few weeks of recovery, the person starts eating better with more and better nutrition than he or she has had in years.

Vitamins, minerals, and herbs are preventative measures to keep us in peak health so problems don't occur. People visit physicians after a problem has uncovered itself, and the physician prescribes medication to help with the problem. The key is to prevent a problem from developing in the first place. Prevention is enhanced with supplements. If the alcoholic can maintain sobriety for a few weeks and lives one step at a time, day by day, then he or she may remain sober. Requirements to maintain sobriety are a desire to stop drinking and a practice of good nutrition with vitamins and mineral supplements.

There are some physicians, nutritionists, psychologists, and psychiatrists who study vitamins, minerals, and herbs. Physicians who know vitamins may also be well versed on the use of nutrition and vitamins in the prevention of alcoholism. There are numerous studies done on the subject, and I agree with them that the educated use of nutrition, vitamins, and the power of the mind can help prevent this disease. If you can see that the mind is a good-versus-bad dilemma, you will understand that a mind that focuses on goodness and those who understand about taking care of themselves would never let alcohol destroy them.

Below are some charts on suggested vitamins, minerals, amino acids, antioxidants, herbs, and natural foods to supplement with nutrition to enhance your health after alcohol abuse. I define alcohol abuse as anything more than one drink or one ounce of alcohol per day.

Essential Vitamins, Minerals, Amino Acids, and Antioxidants to Supplement Nutrition for Health after Alcohol Abuse

Amino Acid Complex	Inositol	Vitamin B complex
GABA	L-Cysteine	Vitamin C
Grape Seed Extract	L-Methionine	Vitamin D
Green Vitamin, Iron Free	Taurine	Vitamin E
Glutathione	Vitamin A	

Important Minerals, Amino Acids, and Antioxidants to Supplement Nutrition for Health after Alcohol Abuse

Alpha Lipoic Acid	Lecithin	Primrose Oil
Calcium	L-Arginine	Raw Liver Extract
Choline	L-Carnitine	Selenium
Kyolic (Aged Garlic)	Magnesium	Zinc

Important Herbs to Supplement Nutrition for Health after Alcohol Abuse

Alfalfa	Burdock Root
Aloe Vera	Silymarin

Important Foods for Health after Alcohol Abuse

Bananas	Garlic or (Kyolic)	Nuts
Beans, All Kinds	Green Vegetables	Prunes
Distilled Water	Kelp	Raisins
Fish	Liver	Rice
Fruits	Molasses	Vegetable Juice

Other nutritional tips:

Change to a more vegetarian diet and reduce red meat from your diet. This will increase energy.

No salt, pepper, coffee, soda, spices, sugar, or flour.

Don't eat butter, cheese, fatty foods, chips, or refined foods.

Drugs put a great strain on the liver, and alcohol increases that stress.

Vitamins A, D, and E are stored in the body. Vitamins B and C aren't stored in the body and are lost daily.

Alcoholics consistently want something pleasurable, but they are never sure what it is they want. This is the mixed thinking of alcoholics, whose bodies tell them they need nutrition, but their minds tell them they need alcohol. Alcoholics will usually succumb to alcohol, because alcohol will stop the hunger and the feeling of wanting nutrition. Many alcoholics are very malnourished and sometimes have bloated stomachs, gastritis, obesity, or extreme thinness due to a total lack of nutrition. An alcoholic can consume alcohol and sweets to the extreme and keep coming back for more. Sweets, on the other hand, play a vital role for the alcoholic who has stopped drinking. After alcohol has ceased and for the next few years, when the desire to drink comes over the person, the trick is to eat a little candy or drink fruit juice, something sweet that will temporarily satisfy the craving for alcohol. The craving will pass. This trick raises the blood sugar level in the system and is especially true for the newly recovering alcoholic.

Cirrhosis of the Liver

Always consult a physician for the correct medication, nutrition, and supplements for use with cirrhosis specific to your individual case. Here is a suggested general protocol for cirrhosis of the liver, a common consequence of drinking alcohol on a consistent basis. Cirrhosis of the liver isn't highly noticeable during drinking; it is subtle. Once drinking stops, a person should get an evaluation from a physician. The liver is the only organ in the body that has the capability to restore itself, to rebuild destroyed parts of the liver if the right medications, nutrition, vitamins, and minerals are taken and the liver hasn't been destroyed beyond repair. If you have drunk for years or decades, always consult a physician to check your physical health, especially your liver. Physicians who specialize in this treatment are very knowledgeable in the use of supplements for cirrhosis, in addition to medication and nutrition.

If cirrhosis of the liver has been diagnosed by a physician, here is the general suggested protocol.

Drink lots of distilled water. Consume almonds, bananas, prunes, raisins, rice, artichokes, wheat bran, vegetables, fruits, beet juice, and carrot juice.

Don't consume meat, fried food, prepared food, or drugs unless prescribed by a physician.

Go on a three-day juice fast, cleansing the liver with a variety of juices, fruits, and vegetables. Eat kidney beans, soy beans, and peas, since these are the only foods that will detoxify ammonia. The other mineral that will detoxify ammonia is manganese. Follow the directions on the bottle.[4]

Essential Vitamins, Minerals, Amino Acids, Antioxidants, and Natural Food Supplements to Supplement with Nutrition for Cirrhosis of the Liver

Alfalfa	Inositol	Magnesium	Taurine
Aloe Vera	Kyolic or Garlic	Manganese	Vitamin B Complex
Chlorophyll	Lecithin	Milk Thistle	Extra B-1, B-6, B-12
Choline	L-Arginine	Multi-Enzyme Complex	Vitamin C
Colostrum	L-Carnitine	Primrose Oil	Vitamin D
CoQ10	L-Cysteine	SAMe	Vitamin E
Folic Acid	Liv-R-Actin	Raw Liver Extract	Vitamin K
Glutathione	L-Methionine	Selenium	Zinc

Most vitamins and minerals can be found in a good vitamin store, online, or via a pharmacy or health food store. Also see appendix B for some suggested vitamin manufactures and distributors.

---

[4] Phyllis A. Balch and James F Balch, *Prescription for Nutritional Healing* (London: Penguin, 2010), 336–340.

Night Blindness

Here is a suggested protocol for night blindness, as stated by Dr. James F. Balch, MD. Alcoholics experience night blindness when they have a hard time seeing light at night and/or when light is too bright, and they cannot see the line on the road or the edge of the road. Night blindness is common in alcoholics who have drunk for a sustained period. [5]

Essential Vitamins, Minerals, Amino Acids, and Antioxidants to Supplement Nutrition for Night Blindness

Amino Acid	Lutein	Vitamin B Complex
Desiccated Liver	Selenium	Vitamin C
Green Source, Iron Free	Taurine	Vitamin E
Glutathione	Vitamin A	Zinc

There are a variety of eye complex vitamins. Check online or any vitamin store for an eye complex vitamin. See the retail vitamin distributor list in appendix B. If you notice night blindness is occurring, consult an ophthalmologist or physician as soon as possible. Vitamins are subtle, and consistency is the key to getting the maximum effect of the vitamin. Follow the direction on the label.

Withdrawal

Always consult a physician when you are ready to stop drinking alcohol. Withdrawal from alcohol can be life threatening by itself, depending on the length of drinking and the reaction of the mind and body to losing the alcohol an alcoholic has learned to cope with and adjust to for so many years. Addiction is both mental and physical, and sometimes the stress of stopping alcohol may lead to death. The most common symptoms in withdrawal are insomnia, nausea, hallucinations, shakes, DTs, high

---

[5] Phyllis A. Balch and James F Balch, *Prescription for Nutritional Healing* (London: Penguin, 2010), 415–429.

sensitivity to light, noise, lack of eating, imbalance, depression, a total loss of self, an inability to function without alcohol, heart problems, stress, a sense of not knowing what to do next, a loss of memory, confusion, and convulsions.

It is recommended that to stop drinking, a physician should be consulted, and this is the reason many alcoholics check themselves into an alcohol treatment facility. Alcoholics, in the majority of cases, cannot stop on their own; they need someone with the knowledge and expertise to help them. It's a matter of treating not only the body from withdrawal and other physical conditions that may erupt but also the mind. A mind coming out of an alcohol fog after years and sometimes decades of drinking, and with the depletion of most or all of the life-giving vitamins and minerals, may be a life-threatening situation. Stopping alcohol is handled best with the needed expertise of physicians practicing in this area or an alcohol treatment facility where a physician is present.

Once a person has gotten through the withdrawal process and is able, counseling starts to take place. Talking with other alcoholics is instrumental in the alcoholic not feeling alone, and other people understand what is wrong with them, and they realize they aren't alone in the world. This is where meetings of Alcoholics Anonymous offer the full benefit of talking with other people who understand you as well as teaching you a program for living.

Treatment is about getting a person back into better physical and mental health. Recovery starts to occur at the same time as treatment. Once the alcohol is taken out of the system, a person begins to heal. Within a few days of treatment, new learning starts to take place not only with nutrition but also with learning new tools to use to overcome the cravings.

Chapter 4

Alcoholism Recovery and Long-Term Maintenance

For recovery to occur, you must open your mind a little and have a willingness to learn something new and a desire to stop drinking. For the most part, people try to make things more secure for themselves. They are habit driven and uneasy with change. As long as you are in control of the change, it becomes a positive thing. When someone else wants to change you, you start asking why, and maybe you exhibit some defiance.

Positive change has to come from within. Education and knowledge are the biggest forces of change. Contemplate what it is you need to learn and then go learn it. Seminars, colleges, and night classes are some of the opportunities you learn from. Learning can be the greatest experience of your life. It is a lifelong job and must be sought out. You have heard that knowledge is power, and it is true. When people learn more than they knew and all the facts support that this something new is good, people may try for it and become empowered. Learning and knowledge provide for more options in life, more choices. Recovery is about learning and change. Recovery is learning new tools to use in life to make better choices.

If you start perfecting things in your life that work and get rid of the things that don't, your life will become better and better.

Part of this process has to do with trying new things. Look at what you need and then seek ways to make that change. Start by recognizing and getting away from negative people in your life. These are people who consume your energy, who don't know how to live on their own, but are constantly taking from you mentally, physically, or financially, referred to as dependence. Stay away from people you don't trust and who aren't honest. Good people are wise; they take nothing from you, and are content with knowing only you, people who support you and your efforts at making a better life. Surround yourself with good people.

Recovery Process

Powerlessness

One of the first steps in recovery is to admit powerlessness over your addiction; admit that the addiction controls you and consumes your thinking and money. Also admit the problems the addiction has caused you. Once you admit powerlessness to yourself, you have overcome a main barrier. Once you admit truthfulness with yourself, the opposite of this being in denial and self-centeredness, you will take your first objective look at yourself and being truthful with yourself. This is the first step to admitting to yourself defeat over something you thought was normal. Just the fact that you're reading this book on this subject means you realize, at least a little, that you may have a problem or at least that something in your life needs to be changed. Just as the disease of alcoholism is progressive, the recovery is progressive. Your recovery progress is contingent upon your spiritual growth.

To give up drinking, one must first admit powerlessness. Admit you are powerless over the alcohol. Admit that alcohol is controlling your life, finances, and all aspects of your thinking. You must surrender the alcohol, surrender yourself to a higher power, God, something more powerful than you. Surrendering is a key to recovery. Powerlessness and surrendering are a mental exercise you do in your mind. Put these thoughts in your mind to begin the process of healing yourself. If you're lacking any spiritual foundation, find something you can call a higher power or God. Define God as you understand him. For example, your God, your higher power might be positive, supportive, forgiving, helpful, and wise. He may love and understand you. Your higher power will provide you with the extra strength and courage to overcome the power of the cravings and the addiction itself. Your higher power will get you through anything in life, in sickness or in health. Use your higher power to help you push these negative thoughts out of your head. The thoughts and cravings will pass.

As you use your higher power, you will gain more self-control and self-discipline. Use the Serenity Prayer often.

> God, grant me the serenity,
> To accept the things I cannot change,
> The courage to change the things I can,
> And the wisdom to know the difference.

Nobody wants to admit complete defeat in his or her life, but with an addiction, this is the first step in overcoming it. Once you have admitted this truth, surrender; then you are ready to move on. If you cannot admit powerlessness over alcohol, then you cannot move on. If you cannot admit complete, 100 percent powerlessness, then you will go on to drink again. Alcohol has probably already controlled much of your life. If you have a 1 percent belief that you can control alcohol, then you have the power to drink again, and you will if you don't admit complete powerlessness over alcohol at this first stage of recovery. You will drink again in a week, a month, a year, or sometime in the future. This concept is highly important in recognizing your choices and understanding that drinking will lead to incomprehensible demoralization or death. Drinking will give you back all the problems you had before. If you don't like a sober lifestyle, life will gladly refund your drinking lifestyle and your problems.

The first time, or the first day you begin to practice powerlessness and surrender, you begin to increase your choices. You will begin to increase your survival instinct. You will begin to decrease the self-destructive acts you have been practicing. For the first time in life, you will have conscious choices, the choices to do or not to do. Choices will become a key factor every day of your life in making a choice not to drink. Soon this choice will become a daily habit, one day at a time. You practice choices one day at a time, sometimes one second at a time.

For the first time in your life, forgive yourself for drinking and stop beating yourself up. Increase the "like yourself" attitude. Like yourself enough to make good choices. Like yourself enough to know you are worth it, that God loves you always. Like yourself enough to take care of you, because nobody else will. Like yourself enough to know you deserve a fair amount of everything good in life: finances, sex, respect, love, happiness, and freedom. Understand that "the more dependence you place on a higher power, the more independent you will be."[6] "Take care of yourself in life, because nobody else will take care of you" (anonymous).

The second process in recovery deals a little more with our thinking—how we think of ourselves, what good things we want for ourselves, what kind of life we really want, what kind of shortfalls we have, what are our weak points are, and whether we are strong enough to be truthful with ourselves.

To stop drinking, the alcoholic must give his or her willpower to a higher power or God. Now you will have help to overcome the cravings, and your choices will now become better choices. Not drinking is a choice. Drinking is a choice. This may sound simple, but if it were that simple, a person could have stopped drinking at any time. Once the "ism" sets in, there is no longer free choice; there is only one choice, and that is to drink. The higher power will allow alcoholics to have a choice once again. Once you practice this choice of not drinking for one day, then one week, and then one month, at some point in time this new practice will become a habit. This is exactly the way alcoholics started drinking, one day at a time, creating a habit. Now a nondrinking choice will happen one day at a time.

Honesty

The second step deals a little more with our thinking, how we think about ourselves. What good things do you want for yourself? And what

---

[6] *Twelve Steps and Twelve Traditions* (New York: Alcoholics Anonymous World Services Inc., 2010), 36.

kind of life do you really want? Success in recovery depends on how truthful you can be to yourself. You are the most important person in your life. Love yourself enough to be truthful with yourself and make good choices. Alcoholics have been in denial for most of their drinking career. For the first time in your life, if you want to stop drinking, become truthful with yourself.

Spirituality

Spirituality is one of the five areas of life, and it is crucial to spend time in this area, also known as faith. This may be one of your greatest and hardest challenges, but the inner reward will be great. It will give you that peace of mind you have been seeking in terms of validating yourself, being at peace with life and death, and continuing to do good things in your life. Alcoholics drink for peace of mind and can now achieve it without alcohol. Once you learn to let go of the past, give your problems to God, and seek inner peace, you will now be able to do good things. A person troubled by divorce, death, or any other life-changing event cannot move on until it has been dealt with. Let go of it, give it to God, and then you are ready to move on in your life.

You can hold onto death, revenge, anger, fear, guilt, or shame forever or until you die. Or you can let go of it today and start living your life again. Holding on to the past will control you, but many people do it; letting go takes some courage, some deep inner decisions, and a desire to make your life better and peaceful again. In the death of a child, parents may hold on to hurt, guilt, shame, or depression for decades; but after spending a reasonable time and making peace with God, this can be accomplished. Keep those good memories. I'm not saying there's anything wrong with holding on, but after a period (and that will be different for everyone), there is a right time to let go, start taking care of yourself, and move forward in life. Holding on to something from the past will control you, in your thinking and your actions. Anger, resentment, grief, guilt, shame, and jealousy are all emotions that will control you if you hold onto them. Let go and let God handle and guide you in these emotions. Letting go means giving the problem, issue, or emotion to God to handle.

Often in life, anger, resentment, or a problem is too much for a person to handle, and it is better left with God to handle. There are many things in life a person is powerless over, and these issues or emotions are better handled by God. An example would be being powerless over the past. People cannot change the past; therefore, they may give to God any shortcomings they may have so God can fix or handle them. They do so because these are too much for a person to handle, and they are now beyond their control. So, give them to God.

An unspiritual person doesn't usually accept religion in one day; it is a process. The point is that church attendance or spiritual learning is a positive activity; it will keep the mind occupied for some time and teach good living in the process. Many recovering alcoholics now find church to be their savior from alcohol. Church or spiritual activities can bring peace of mind alcoholics have never experienced in their lifetimes. Shop around for the church, spiritual activity, or positive-living program you like. Whatever process works for you is the key. There isn't one right answer, but whatever works for you to stay sober is the best answer. Spirituality gives you faith, grace, and hope. And with that you get peace of mind.

Meditation

Meditation can be described as a state of conscious mind just before sleep; it's a state of mind that is totally void of all thought but conscious of one focal point, in which the whole body is in a relaxation state. It's a place where the person is in complete control of his or her mind. In the beginning, people can keep all thoughts out of their minds for a short period. As more practice takes place, the period of time can be extended. If they can maintain this state of mind for a minimal period of time and the period gradually increases, they will soon experience a tremendous burst of energy as they begin their daily routine again. With practice, someone will begin to use this technique maybe more than once per day. If the stress level is high, a person experienced in meditation can stop at any time, take two to five minutes, and push all thoughts and stress away, bringing the mind back down to a totally relaxed level. He or she can then pick one task and start again, with a much clearer mind and more energy than before. Once this technique is perfected, it can have many uses, and the person will learn how to use them to his or her advantage.

This technique is particularly helpful to alcoholics, who can now push thoughts of drinking, cravings, or negative thoughts out of their heads at any given moment in time. So meditation is a key tool an alcoholic may use to quiet those thoughts. I have seen a lot of good teachings in alcohol recovery programs, such as prayer, but I sometimes don't see the use of meditation. There are no pills or drugs, just the power of the body to relax itself and quiet the mind, if one knows the technique. Meditation is a key tool to use for long-term recovery.

What I have generally seen more of is the use of prayer as meditation. There is a distinct difference between prayer and meditation. I define prayer as seeking guidance from a higher power or God, and meditation is an emptying or quietness of the mind. A certain percentage of alcohol treatment and recovery is short term, and the reason is that while many good things are taught. There are still many tools available such as nutrition, supplements and meditation. Both are key tools for long-term recovery. Many people use the AA program or a positive-living program for life, and it works, but the people who relapse and keep going in and out of recovery, need it most. Meditation is sometimes referred to as prayer. Sometimes prayer and meditation are interactive and relational. Both should be used in a program of recovery.

A good percentage of alcoholics constantly think and overthink. Sometimes they may do little, but there is a lot of thinking going on up there. One main excuse or reason for drinking is to help people sleep. Alcoholics seem to have an excess amount of extra thinking above what they need to survive. They always have these great ideas, schemes, inventions, arguments with themselves and others, or reactions to something somebody said two days or two months ago. If it hurt them, they are still thinking about it.

This is one of the reasons so many alcoholics get themselves into trouble; too many times they cannot differentiate between past and present, right and wrong, and they are always crossing the line. They operate in the extreme, just like their thinking. In this sense meditation is the great savior of many alcoholics. A sentence a judge should add to the first drinking offense is to learn meditation, because the humiliation and embarrassment of picking up trash for community service works in a negative way; learning meditation would be a positive step in preventing drinking offenses a second time. Teach the offender how to push out or stop thoughts of drinking. This learning works in a positive way.

It has been my experience that once recovering alcoholics learn this technique, it's a tool they can use for life when the cravings start. Cravings are usually caused by a nutritional imbalance. An alcoholic may start the meditation and bring reality back into perspective. There is a saying that says, "Think, think, think." This means you only get three thinks; if you haven't resolved your issue by the third think, stop thinking about it and give it to God to handle.

Change

Alcoholics really get excited at the thought of having fun in the extreme, just like their drinking and overthinking. When it comes to having fun, the alcoholic seems to like extreme. I attribute this to the fact that many alcoholics may have had too much responsibility at an early age, or they had to go to work at an early age or grow up very quickly. When you stop life short and skip developmental steps and processes, problems start to manifest themselves. If people can begin to achieve a balance of work and play, then they will accomplish a balance. Often alcoholics are missing limits, boundaries, and balance in their lives. They spend either too much time working (workaholics) or too much time not working.

Changes can mean many different things, from nutrition to supplements, exercise, or a willingness to take care of oneself. It can mean a change in the way you think about the past or look at your upbringing and the thinking and tools you were given as a child. It can mean a change in the way you look at things or treat people, or it can be a change in your morals, values, and beliefs. There can also be a change in your dress, your motives, and your positive thinking. You can have a realistic, positive way of looking at your differences or weak points, or there can be a change in the way you view the world and God. Or there could be a change in what you read, what you watch on TV, or where you spend your time. You may change your choices.

A change in lifestyle means many different things for different people. Some may want to change a lot, others a little. Sometimes once you change a few things, many other changes will follow. Actions are the key to a lifestyle change. Being around positive people and actions while eliminating negative people and actions from your life is a main key to recovery and success.

Regarding change, if you have a reputation as an alcoholic, eight years will need to pass for people to forget your old drinking personality, habits, and reputation. It takes time for other people to realize you are acting differently or that you are a nicer different person than you used to be. Change is a process, just as it was a process for you to build a drinking reputation; now it is a process to project you are a different person. This is a psychological phenomenon that reminds you to protect your reputation. It takes time to build a good, respectful, trusting reputation.

Nutrition is a real key factor in mental and physical chemical balance. As you age, your vitamins, minerals, and hormones begin to decrease. You cannot eat enough to raise those levels to your thirty-year-old level. This is where nutritional supplements come in. Vitamins will help you raise those levels to your thirty-year-old level. Also, in regard to nutrition, the more you move toward a vegetarian diet, the more energy you'll have. You don't have to go to the extreme, but the more vegetarian you become and the less red meat you eat, the healthier you should feel. Nutrition and exercise are basic key elements in a lifestyle change.[7]

---

[7] Gary Null, *Gary Null's Ultimate Anti-Aging Program* (New York: Kensington, 1999), 6, 313, 316.

Exercise is a key to physical well-being. All work and exercise are respectable. Take some time to provide yourself with some exercise, whether it's as simple as walking or as complex as going to a gym.

Once you become complacent in life, you may stay that way for years or decades, or until something jolts you into a change. As for alcoholics, what usually changes them is that their lives keep getting worse and worse until at some point they have had enough and want to do something about it. Many act out the change in a negative way, which may land them in jail, but some start acting out in a positive way, and those who ask for help are the ones who usually succeed. Some never get the message, and many alcoholics die of alcohol-related diseases, insanity, or a combination of both as their lives deteriorate more and more.

Character Defects

Character defects are defined as an action or non-action that can be improved. Character defects don't mean a person is defective. For example, if alcoholics are in denial that alcohol is hurting their family, the character defect is their inability to see how they are hurting family members. To fix this defect, alcoholics need to be more truthful with themselves by realizing that money spent on alcohol is taking away from the family. Drinking alcohol may also make the person more reactive to family members, and the improvement would be how to be a nicer person and someone not so reactive. A character defect pertains to an action that can be approved on.

Look at your character defects. Are you a nice person? Do you have positive thinking all the time? Do you try to do good most of the time, or do you slip for one hour a day or more and gossip or hate someone or want to get even or get mad at something somebody said? Do you participate in gossip, or are you focused on yourself and doing good things for yourself, disregarding all gossip or comments other people make? Are you a good spouse and parent, or can your behavior be improved upon? Did the boss reprimand you for something unfairly? It wasn't your fault or your responsibility. How did you handle it? Did you react or discuss it? Do you function in the extreme, in pride, greed, lust, envy, gluttony, anger, or fear at any time? There is a saying I see hanging in many places today: "Your attitude is the only thing you are in control of today," and I add "for the alcoholic every second of the day."

Identifying character defects allows people to improve on them. Character defects may also be described as weak points or shortcomings. When people make a concerted effort to fix their weak points or character defects, they become better people. Identifying your character defects is a key tool in recovery and long-term maintenance, and it becomes a life-time job. What can you do better today than yesterday?

What things in your personality can you improve on? Can you be a better friend, a better spouse, a better parent, or a better employee? This kind of thinking allows for a lifetime of improvement. For the alcoholic who has created a lot of hurt and wreckage in the past, the process will help him or her make the most progress in living life on life's terms.

Admit your character defects to yourself and another trusted human being.

Character defects usually fall in the area of the seven sins: pride, greed, lust, gluttony, anger, sloth, and envy. They may manifest themselves in our present actions or morals or through the use of words or actions. Once alcoholics are ready, they need to admit their character defects to themselves and another trusted human being. Once this takes place, a burden will be lifted from the alcoholics, and now they will be free to work on or improve on those characteristics rather than carry them around as guilt or shame. Many alcoholics have many good traits, such as big hearts, giving attitudes, hardworking attributes, helping personalities, and many others.

For alcoholics to stop drinking, they must verbally admit their defects and wrongdoings to themselves and another trusted person. When alcoholics take on this challenge, it is like taking a personal life inventory. Where have they wronged or hurt other people? Are they too greedy, too lustful, a messy person, a miser, a big shot? Are they angry or envious, wanting more of everything? Once alcoholics admit these defects and wrongdoings, they can move ahead in the process of recovery.

You are the most important person in your life. You are an important person, and whether you know it, you are probably a leader for someone else. In someone's eyes, you may be a leader, whether it be a family group, a child, a work group, friends, or maybe a younger person you know who looks up to you or admires you, and you may not know it. So remember that you are important to you; do good things for yourself always. This is an extremely important process in recovery. Lead by example.

Humility

Here is a definition of humility from the teachings of Bill W., who founded Alcoholics Anonymous. He kept this plaque on his desk about humility: "Humility is perpetual quietness of heart. It is to have no trouble. It is never to be fretted or vexed, irritable or sore, to wonder at nothing that is done to me, to feel nothing done against me. It is to be at rest when nobody praises me, and when I am blamed or despised, it is to have a blessed home in myself where I can go and shut the door and kneel to my God in secret and be at peace, as in a deep sea of calmness, when all around and about is seeming trouble."[8]

Remain humble always, because humility is a character asset. If you go through life not expecting anything from anybody and have nothing to prove to anybody, this attitude will give you peace of mind. When you have peace of mind, you can make better choices. One of the main reasons alcoholics drink is to find peace of mind. Don't get hung up in "big shotism," thinking you are better, more important, or smarter than anybody else. This could also be envying or wanting what everybody else has. Try to carry a good attitude with you for the rest of the day. If you find yourself getting negative, meditate briefly, push all thoughts out of your head, and try again. Do one thing at a time, one

---

[8] *Alcoholics Anonymous* (New York: Alcoholics Anonymous World Services Inc., 2001) Bill W (anonymous).

conversation at a time. With practice you can maintain this positive attitude for longer periods of time. Stay away from negative people and negative situations that make you uncomfortable. Humility is a key tool in maintaining long-term sobriety.

Daily and monthly, look back and see where you have succeeded and failed. If you have failed, how can you do better tomorrow? Admit when you are wrong. Pray each morning to do good, and be thankful each night about the good you have accomplished. Be thankful for everything in your life.

Attitude

One of the most important aspects in recovery is attitude. There is only one thing in life you can control, and that is your attitude. From the time you get up in the morning, you have a choice about your attitude every second of the day.

Alcoholics are notorious for negative attitudes. They are fierce reactors, and they can mentally hurt people when they talk. They may be constantly craving alcohol or are in the state of a hangover. Alcoholics aren't always the nicest people to be around. They may always blame others for all their failures in life—"Poor me," "Feel sorry for me"—with extremely negative attitudes. Once sobriety takes hold in two days or two months, they may start to take control of their attitudes. Say a prayer first thing in the morning to do good things. When you come in contact with others, make sure it is a positive experience for the other person. Here are some other tips that may help.

When you talk to others, use good words; if you have a tendency to use foul language, many people find foul language offensive when they are trying to talk to you. They may not say anything at the time, but they will stop listening to you. Use good language that is appropriate for the listener. Be pleasant and positive. If you have stopped drinking and are still using foul language, then your tongue is still out of control, just as your drinking was. As more progress is made in a recovery program and the desire to do good and get new learning sets in, the foul language decreases.

Look at the situations you will encounter that day. Avoid negative situations and negative people. They will try to bring you into their world. Look at the situations you will face that day and think them out, understanding that things may not go your way. Don't react but listen, and you will learn. Listen for mutual understanding. Be prepared to voice your opinion and explain why it is better, with facts. Listen, and then when it is time, you may say your opinion in a positive manner; speak so the listener can understand.

Attitude should be practiced and perfected for a lifetime. Look at what works and what doesn't. Ask yourself that question; you will know that answer yourself. Strive to improve yourself, your vocabulary, and your meet-and-deal qualities. If you are a recovering alcoholic and have been drinking for some years, your vocabulary and thinking capacity will be limited, but you may not recognize this. Other people will. So take this suggestion slowly; it takes practice, learning, and more talking to build up your vocabulary to the level where you used to be along with your listening skills.

As you practice a positive attitude, being positive will become easier. Push yourself to go to positive events and places where you may practice humility, which is the opposite of what you were doing when you were drinking. Force yourself to get into new good activities, including reading, writing, social and cultural events, education, learning, a new business, or spiritual learning. Find something good, something you like.

Some of the best education and reading you can do means starting with some self-help books about health, nutrition, personality, meditation, or self-actualization. Those who take an interest in their health are on their way to a better life; health is the first step, which leads into all other areas of your life. Life is divided into those five areas: career, family, spiritual, psychological, and physiological. Spend a little time in each, and you will see your life coming into balance. When an alcoholic takes time to drink, he or she takes away from all of the five areas. If one is drinking, there is less time with the family and probably little to no spiritual emphasis, no psychological emphasis, and probably no physiological emphasis. No alcohol or any illegal drug or negative activity fits into one of the five areas of life.

The first year of sobriety is like a feel-good elation in itself, as newfound recovering alcoholics get their senses back. The fog clears from their heads, and reality becomes excessively real. This has to do with the exaggerated awareness that recovering alcoholics have and their heightened instincts they have acquired from their alcoholic living in a fog for so long. The senses and instincts had to function at a higher level just to keep the alcoholics alive, since their actions were self-destructive. When sobriety sets in, the instincts stay, and as far as I can tell, this heightened awareness may last for some time. I have seen alcoholics become very good intellectual thinkers after years of sobriety. Many times they have great insight into deep thought and some of the unanswered questions in life. This is partly due to the fact that they spent so much time in deep thinking while they were drinking, trying to answer and figure out questions about life and death (What came first, the chicken or the egg? Is there really a God?) Acceptance is the answer to many of life's questions.

As sobriety sets in, drinkers experience total shock to the mind and body before they start feeling comfortable while living again without alcohol. This process can take days or weeks. I have also seen on numerous occasions, after a short period of sobriety, that recovering alcoholics are able to see both sides of everything. For example, they can now see joy versus sadness, good versus bad, dependence versus independence, kindness versus selfishness; they now know freedom as well as addiction. They now become very well-rounded, thinking individuals with great insight and compassion into many situations.

I have seen time after time that once sobriety sets in, the brain has to start using new paths to re-learn old tasks and thinking, since alcoholism destroyed some of those old normal paths. Once relearning starts taking place, the brain has to use a new path to relearn. Everything becomes a new experience. This is true for many things the alcoholic knew how to do while drinking; now he or she has to relearn sober.

The upside of this is that everything becomes new to alcoholics, just as if they were young again, and the learning and experiencing start all over again. This is an amazing process to watch, since alcoholics who already had an overabundance of zest for living still have that overabundance of zest while sober. Alcoholics can be a joy in sobriety. Many maintain this extra energy in everything they do. This is one of the reasons an employer who maintains an alcoholic through recovery gains it all back, plus more, in sobriety. As alcoholics make new friends, they usually maintain these friendships since they now become a person that people like.

Alcoholics who used to function on the negative side now become positive, and as those brain waves make a new path for themselves, they become somewhat different thinking people. In my experience, the brain now mediates those extreme personalities to something more of a level pattern that generally makes for a nicer person. As they learn more and get more sober experience, they tend to lose the extreme actions and thinking in their behavior. Recovering alcoholics no longer operate on the edge or in the extreme as they did for many years. Some of this learning can come naturally, but most comes from working some type of positive recovery program.

The real test for a recovering alcoholic comes years after sobriety, after much of the new learning has taken place and after the first year when everything is new. Then in the second year, a little more reality sets in, and in the third year, when alcoholics are truly in reality, the damage from their past becomes very clear. They will sink or swim on any given day. Many still suffer from highs and lows, sometimes daily. At this point, I'm not going to cover the relapse back into drinking but only the sobriety. If sobriety continues to progress, adding in new things such as studying something new or finding new careers, any long-term positive goal that can keep the alcoholic mind busy, is a key to success. This will be a key point to remember in all the following years. Alcoholics must continue to do good things, because once boredom sets in, a drink is highly likely. Most alcoholics have very busy minds, and it is to their benefit to keep the mind busy. They must now be aware of focusing on something they like to do and do it. If they are stuck in jobs or lifestyles they don't particularly like, it's all the more important that they do something they like for the rest of their lives.

One important characteristic in recovery is how one thinks. Here are some thinking patterns needed for success. Alcoholics need to let go of much of their learned behavior as children and adults. If they also had drinking parents, they should probably forget almost everything they ever learned from them.

Keep in mind that you are just a regular person, nothing more and nothing less. You are a person God loves. No matter what you thought you were or could be, now look at what you really are in sobriety. You are just a regular person. Look at the damage around you that you have caused to you, your spouse, your kids, family members, your business associates, employers, or the people who work for you. All those people have feelings you have probably hurt at one time or another.

Ask yourself why your spouse stayed with you through all these years of drinking. Why didn't your spouse leave when he or she should have? Ask yourself whether you have taken care of your spouse and kids the best you could. I want to add at this point that the answer to this last question is yes, because alcoholics did the best they could with what they knew while they were drinking. What they don't realize is that because of drinking, lack of information, and ignorance, they could have done better. The money spent on alcohol could have been spent on better things in life. Alcoholics don't need to take on any more guilt. For years they thought they did the best they could. But as sobriety sets in and more information and choices are visible to them, they soon realize they could have done better.

Alcoholics are people, too, and they are usually more sensitive than most people. They will shed many a tear as the realization sets in of how many people they have hurt and of how they have hurt themselves. There's a funny thing about the mind; it won't let in too much information and awareness in at one time. If it didn't withhold some awareness, the shock would be too great for anyone to bear. But the mind will let in a little awareness at a time to adjust the behavior a little at a time.

Once alcoholics get through the first few weeks of sobriety, new learning starts taking place. If a nutritional plan is followed, then learning will be much easier, since the body won't focus on nutritional needs alone. If nutritional needs aren't met, learning will be slow as the body and mind concentrate on meeting those needs first. This follows the concept of Maslow's hierarchy of needs and self-actualization, in which basics such as food, shelter, and clothing must first be met before a person can move to a higher level of living, referred to as "self-actualization" or being the best person you can be in life.

Once nutritional needs are met, the next step is to have a few tools to satisfy the craving. There is a saying that "it is better to be overweight, than to be drinking alcohol" (anonymous). When the craving sets in, a few items will satisfy it; one is a little candy, and the other is fruit juice. Have plenty on hand and make them readily available for the newly sober person. Due to a chemical imbalance when the sugar level drops, a craving sets in, which the alcoholic immediately wants to satisfy with alcohol, because alcohol will stop this craving immediately. It will kill the pain. Instead, sugar and fruit juice will satisfy the craving, and the craving will pass.

Alcoholics aren't familiar with dealing with their emotions or feelings and will spend the next years trying to sort out feelings and emotions that have been suppressed for years or decades.

Alcoholics in general are reactors to people. Now they must learn how to function and live without the alcohol and deal with people on life's terms. This is a lifelong task for the nondrinking person, but alcoholics, no matter their age when they get sober, must now learn how to live with themselves and deal with other people while sober. They will learn not to react but rather to discuss. Their defensiveness toward people will disappear as they learn more and become more comfortable with themselves.

If you start perfecting things in your life that work and get rid of the things that don't, your life will become better and better. Part of this sentence has to do with trying new things. Look at what you need and then seek ways to make that change. In the beginning of sobriety, it's best to stay away from drinking friends, relatives, or business associates until you're strong enough to be around these people. You may still have cravings, but you may not have enough tools to overcome a drink. The obsession to drink will disappear, and as more time goes on and you learn more tools, you may be able to be around drinking situations and not be tempted by the drinking.

Anyone familiar with the AA program knows it is a program that should be practiced for a lifetime. Some people may substitute a religious program or some other positive program, but AA teaches a way of living without alcohol every alcoholic understands. The ultimate key here is to practice whatever works for you. Many people try to stop drinking, and a certain percentage will succeed. If the positive program is stopped, then old thinking seems to set back in, usually with fatal results. Even alcoholics with lots of years of sobriety will experience this concept if they stop practicing a positive-living program. The old thinking comes back, and alcoholics will justify and convince themselves that they can take a drink again. It's so important that alcoholics keep learning and practicing their new program so they stay away from negative thoughts, such as, *I'm special. I deserve a drink* or *I can handle just one drink.* Alcoholics will need all the self-esteem they can muster in the beginning, since this will carry them through many a hard night. It takes only one second to decide to have another drink, so the more tools alcoholics have to use, the better off they will be to overcome a craving.

When you stop drinking, you will have experienced a miracle from God, and you will know it. This can be described as a very good, light feeling, a feeling of accomplishment. Once you have experienced the miracle, you will want to keep it forever. The burden of alcohol has been lifted off your back. Generally, what happens is that once you have eliminated most or all of the bad from your life and are now putting in what's good, you will have achieved some level of a spiritual awakening or miracle. All alcoholics I have ever spoken with, who have some sober time and are working a positive recovery program, know exactly when and where they experienced the spiritual awakening; they all know a miracle has happened. A spiritual awakening may be described as a place where alcoholics know they are now children of God or a higher power, that they are loved, that their past has been forgiven, and that now they are on a good path with positive things to offer. A miracle may be described as alcoholics knowing that the obsession to drink has been lifted, that the cravings are gone. They are good people and loved by God or a higher power; they now have good things to teach others, and their future is positive. This is described as the miracle.

Triggers

Triggers are defined as people, places, or things that may start the alcoholic drinking again. Recovering alcoholics should avoid negative people, places, and things. They should avoid all people who are going to drink and places where alcohol is available or drinking is taking place. That could be social events, grocery stores that sell alcohol, restaurants with bars, drinking business meetings, or family gatherings if alcohol is present. In the beginning the alcoholics should avoid any place where alcohol is available. Until they get stronger, the least amount of alcohol could trigger temptation and failure. Each individual needs to identify his or her triggers. These are usually referred to as "slippery places." In the beginning some extreme alcoholics even need to avoid any mouthwash, food products, or anything that may have the smallest amount of alcohol in it.

This advice may sound extreme, but I cannot emphasize enough that the smallest amount of alcohol can trigger drinking. Recovering alcoholics need to avoid any temptation until they know they are strong enough to overcome it. I once heard a person in a positive-living program with thirty-five years of sobriety say, they carry a thimble in their pocket to remind them that if they drink as little as a thimble full of alcohol, the misery will start all over again because they won't be able to stop. A recovering alcoholic should pay particular attention to this wisdom.

Cravings

Cravings are defined as a mental or physical need for something. The cravings can be mental or physical. Alcoholism is a mental obsession with alcohol and a physical addiction to it. Cravings diminish when alcohol is stopped, and as new tools are learned, the mental obsession will disappear—sometimes slowly, sometimes quickly. The same is true for the physical addiction as better nutrition and/or supplements are taken; the physical addiction will soon disappear. When the body is deficient of specific vitamins or minerals, it starts craving, usually food, but the alcoholic has learned to eliminate those cravings by consuming alcohol. As good nutrition is practiced, the physical cravings will leave.

There is a saying that goes along with cravings. "This too shall pass." If you experience an alcohol craving, try some sugar or fruit juice and/or read this book. The craving will pass. Cravings can last weeks, months, or even years. When you replace them with something good and positive, they will disappear.

Relapse

I always refer to relapse as someone who wants to drink more than he or she wants to be sober. Any person who doesn't drink and is working a program of recovery but drinks again is said to have relapsed. The individual may call a relapse one drink, one drinking episode, or multiple drinking episodes. Many times an individual will stop drinking and get back into his or her recovery program or routine. There are individuals who have stopped drinking on their own and aren't drinking, but they haven't changed anything else in their lives. They are the same people they were when drinking; they just aren't drinking today. They haven't introduced any new learning or tools to help them not drink; they are abstaining by willpower. I refer to people who relapse as "people who are going to do what they want to do, when they want to do it," referring to self-will. The best predictor of future behavior is past behavior. For recovery, alcoholics have to work a rigorous recovery program. They must want sobriety more than anything else.

To the person who consistently relapses or has relapsed multiple times, who just cannot stop drinking, this behavior is referred to as chronic brain relapse syndrome. These individuals are incapable of being honest with themselves. No truth comes out of the mouths of some people. They are constantly lying to themselves or someone else. The truth for these individuals is only in their actions. Only their actions speak the truth.

Treatment for chronic brain relapse syndrome is long term, nine months or more of disciplined treatment, when there is absolutely no chance of getting alcohol and an individual has to be retaught how to live. These individuals are hard-core drinkers—in fact, hard-core individuals—who will drink even at the cost of financial destruction, family destruction, and homelessness. These individuals must relearn how to live, using all the tools provided in this book. Sometimes these individuals learn through the AA program, some through a religious program such as church, and some through a long-term treatment facility, where they are literally continuously monitored during this nine-month or more period and retaught how to live by using consistent, good habits.

Relapse has no rule, whether you are sober one week or thirty years; a relapse can occur. This is a choice an individual makes to have another drink. Despite all they know, despite what they learned in recovery, they choose to drink again. This fact illustrates the subtle and powerful addiction of alcohol. *Choice* is a key word in recovery; it is a powerful word, one that shouldn't be taken lightly. It is one of the most important words a recovering alcoholic can learn.

Relapse is the biggest heartbreak of all to the family, the employer, and the alcoholic. The fact is, many alcoholics will pursue alcohol into jails, hospitals, poverty, homelessness, and even death. If you relapse, pick up the book and start again. Relapse is not an option.

How does an alcoholic prevent a relapse? Maintaining a healthy mind, body, and spirit is a key to relapse prevention. The alcoholic must make sobriety his or her main priority in life while living one day at a time. For the alcoholic, one drink is too much, and twenty drinks aren't enough. Not taking that first drink is mandatory. Alcoholics must want to stay sober more than they want to drink. Being humble, truthful with yourself, and thankful for what you have is key. Maintaining a dependent relationship on a higher power is contingent on sobriety. Relapse is a one-second choice to have a drink. Relapse prevention comes from within the individual. Recovery is progressive and is contingent upon spiritual growth. There are many tools to use to prevent relapse, such as attending church; going to counseling; working on and maintaining a positive-living program like Alcoholics Anonymous; partnering with a life coach, mentor, or sponsor; and calling someone before the person takes the first drink. Relapse is one of the mysteries of the disease. Why does a person who has a thousand tools to use not to drink one day decide to have a drink, knowing all the negative consequences of alcoholism and having experienced all of them? Why does this person still have one more drink? He or she drinks for that mental numbness, the glow when everything in the world is okay, and for the fantasy of feeling good. Relapse prevention can be accomplished if an alcoholic wants it.

A relapse is more likely if drinking people try to stop drinking on their own. They may muster up enough willpower to stop drinking, but now they are just people with the same personality who stopped drinking. What is highly recommended is that the person should learn the tools from a positive-living program. All the necessary tools are provided in this book. These are tools to avoid having that first drink in the future. An alcoholic seldom recovers on his or her own for the long term.

That's why it's so important for the alcoholic to recognize the goodness of sobriety and keep trying, never giving up. If alcoholics can get truthful with themselves and learn, then the miracle will happen. Each glow from drinking lasts only a short time, whereas being sober and feeling good can last a lifetime.

Groups

The world is made up of groups of all kinds, all waving their arms and saying, "Come and be part of our group." Some groups are subtler. There are family groups, work groups, spiritual groups, shopping groups, social groups, just groups for any and all reasons. Pick your groups carefully and make sure their thinking and goals are good for you. If you ever notice, alcoholics socialize with other alcoholics, because they are in their own group. No one wants to be part of that group except another drinker. Recovering alcoholics are another group; you sure won't find them spending too much time with drinking people, and if you do, more than likely they will also soon be drinking.

All recovering alcoholics have a common unique goal to stay sober. In the beginning, a recovering alcoholic may or may not be able to be around drinking people. Alcoholics generally don't know how to function outside their drinking group, but a recovering alcoholic soon learns how to function in a normal group. Many times a recovering alcoholic with some sober time, can only be around drinking people for a short period of time, and soon learns to distance himself or herself from drinking activities. Therefore, recovering alcoholics should choose their groups carefully.

This is also true for the alcoholic family. Neither children of alcoholics nor alcoholics themselves know how to function outside their environment, and when children try to leave the family, they tend to search for groups they are familiar with, which are drinking groups. They have little experience about how to function in a nondrinking group. See the chapter on "Alcoholism in the Family." There we get into the subject of adult children of alcoholics, who may be nondrinking. They are toned down quite a bit, but they still have some of the character traits they learned all their lives from the drinking parent. Many carry this thinking throughout life, because they fit in just enough to get by, and many do well; they don't seem to have too many problems, depending on what they learned or didn't learn as children.

Children from an alcoholic family will often leave the alcoholic family only to go out and marry an alcoholic. A lot of these people end up in divorces and counseling; or, if they recognize the problem, they seek out organizations such as Adult Children of Alcoholics, or Al-anon, or some other positive-living teachings or educational groups. Adult children of alcoholics often struggle to fit in, and they are quite comfortable with a drinking group, because it is what they are use to. Choose your groups carefully, make sure their agendas and goals are good, and stick with winners.

Alcohol Distorts the Truth

In relationship to alcohol and sex, alcohol can be a sexual stimulant to many drinking people, contrary to public opinion. Some people react differently to alcohol, and maybe to some people, it is a sexual depressant. Alcoholics seem to be wired differently, and alcohol seems to be a stimulant to sex. Whether alcohol is a sexual stimulant or depressant, it lowers one's inhibitions; people do things they wouldn't normally do while sober.

Alcohol impairs or distorts feelings, emotions, judgments, and the truth. When drinking drivers have an accident, their judgement is impaired. There is also a very controversial fine line regarding sexual misconduct when alcohol is involved. Once alcohol is consumed, feelings, emotions, words, desires, common sense, judgment, perceptions, morals, values, beliefs, and truths are all now distorted. When it comes to anything where alcohol is involved, alcohol distorts reality in both males and females, and it always distorts the truth.

Addiction Free

The final process in recovery has to do with living a life that is addiction free, a nondrinking lifestyle. You can help others by using the knowledge you have gained in and after recovery and by continuing to live a better life for yourself. This is a healthy, good life, where you feel good about yourself and the things you do, being proud of what you do and who you are, and being thankful for the gift you have been given mentally, physically, and spiritually. You are now addiction free and have a choice on whether you do the addiction again. The greatest aspect of recovery is that a person has overcome a life-threatening disease. This is a proud but humble accomplishment of all recovering alcoholics. A great gift an alcoholic receives in the process is that he or she now can become the teacher, a leader. Good leaders lead by example.

Part of recovery is sharing what you have learned with the alcoholic who still suffers. This same process can be seen in cancer survivors, who now become cancer counselors; because they are grateful to have overcome cancer, they have the knowledge and experience, and they now want to help the person who has cancer. Through counseling, teaching, and maybe giving rides for the cancer patients, they are giving back and sharing their gift of cancer survivor knowledge. You can also see this process in grief counseling, where someone who has overcome the loss of a loved one is now able to share his or her experience, strength, and hope with another person who has recently lost a loved one. This same process works with alcoholics. By giving back, people are thankful for the gift they have received in recovery and are willing to share their gift and knowledge with someone who is still suffering.

This process also gives the alcoholic a lifetime job of practicing recovery. By talking about their experience, strength, and hope on a continuing long-term basis, alcoholics can make their own recovery a habit on a day-by-day basis for a lifetime. This is a real key to recovery, having empathy for the alcoholic who still suffers and helping those who suffer just as they were helped.

Summary of the Five Processes Suggested for Treatment and Recovery

- Recognize you have a problem and admit powerlessness and defeat over the addiction; give up trying to fight the addiction. Completely surrender yourself to a higher power or God.
- Start being truthful with yourself. Use a treatment center, physician, support group, or trusted friend to help you overcome the addiction.

- Admit your character defects to yourself and another trusted human being. Rely on a higher power to help you overcome the addiction and your character defects.

- Start to recognize the difference between right and wrong, taking care of yourself and doing good things for yourself. Understand cravings, practice nutrition, and learn. Maintain a high awareness that you now have choices.

- The last process has to do with living a life that is addiction free, helping others by using the knowledge you have gained, and continuing to live a life for yourself, a healthy, good life, where you feel good about yourself and the things you do. Be proud of what you do and who you are and be thankful for the gift you have been given mentally, physically, and spiritually. Now you are addiction free and have a choice on whether you do the addiction again.

It is a well-known fact that no real alcoholic ever recovers alone. Alcoholics recover only by the grace of God, an intervention by God, a personal conversation with him, or a moment of being touched by him. Every alcoholic must reach a place where he or she has had enough; he or she wants to live and doesn't want to hurt himself or herself or other people anymore. So only by the grace of God does an alcoholic lose the obsession and reach a point called "recovery." With this change, the alcoholic must now strive to practice goodness, wellness, thankfulness, and humility. The alcoholic should now strive to become like the St. Francis Prayer.

> Lord, make me a channel of thy peace—that where there is hatred, I may bring love—that where there is a wrong, I may bring the spirit of forgiveness—that where there is discord, I may bring harmony—that where there is error, I may bring truth—that where there is doubt, I may bring faith—that where there is despair, I may bring hope—that where there are shadows, I may bring light—that where there is sadness, I may bring joy. Lord, grant that I may seek rather to comfort than to be comforted—to

understand, than to be understood—to love, than to be loved. For it is by self-forgetting that one finds. It is by forgiving that one is forgiven. It is by dying that one awakens to Eternal Life. Amen.

It is only by the grace of God that the alcoholic has now been given a second chance at life, a chance to walk in God's image, a chance to become whole and do good things, on a day-by-day basis, by the grace of God. This is referred to as the miracle.

Alcoholic Brain Function

Here is a medical process you may have witnessed that I have seen time and time again in many recovering alcoholics. After decades of drinking, killing brain cells with each drink, six days a week, fifty-two weeks a year, for many years or decades, a significant number of brain cells are destroyed, and brain cells cannot replace themselves. The amount of functioning reaches a crisis point, since the remaining functioning brain cells decrease as more drinking occurs. As this happens, bodily functions decline subtly. This isn't noticeable on a day-to-day or even month-to-month basis, but it can be noticed on a year-to-year basis. Many drinking people attribute it to old age, along with symptoms such as declining memory; occasional loss of bladder or bowel control; loss of strength or mobility; quirky thinking; flare-ups of anger, agitation, or nervousness; a condition of being less and less relaxed; thinking that is a little off the norm; and a state of being somewhat negative.

This is the thinking that leads to insanity in alcoholics. The decline is there, but it is very subtle and slow, and it's hardly noticeable over the years. After a person has been drinking alcohol for years or decades and then stops, the amazing brain, through rehabilitation and repetitive actions, can relearn. This fact has been proven time and time again, especially with accident and stroke victims, through rehabilitation. The simple explanation is that the brain begins to relearn how to function in a closely related part of the brain. If a specific activity is normally done with the small section of the brain and that section decreases with more and more alcohol consumption, that activity becomes more and more difficult. When the drinking stops, after days or weeks of confusion, the brain will revert to a closely related part of the brain. Through repetition, the relearning process begins and continues.

I have witnessed this condition time and time again, especially in barely functioning alcoholics. This process is referred to as brain plasticity. People who cannot walk after an accident learn to walk. People who cannot use an arm after a stroke learn to use the arm again through repetitive actions and workouts, and they relearn. A stroke victim, in whom a little part of the brain has died and who cannot move an arm or talk correctly, can many times correct the arm or speech through repetitive exercise and repetitive practice. Alcoholics use this same principle through mental exercise, repetitive thinking, and physical activity; they can relearn to think and function again once the alcohol stops. Talking and thinking will be corrected through brain plasticity as well as practice, repetition, and relearning. Dr. Frank Lawless describes this process in his book *Not My Child: A Progressive and Proactive Approach for Healing Addicted Teenagers and Their Families.* This is the same process that happens to alcoholics when they stop drinking; the brain rewires itself to gain back what it lost through years of continuous drinking. It's like the brain transfers what little information it has left and transfers it to a related part of the brain. The learning process begins anew and continues through learning and repetition of day-to-day activities and habits, including talking and thinking. This is referred to as brain plasticity. [9]

Below is an anonymous alcoholic's spiritual story of success.

An Alcoholic's Spiritual Story

An alcoholic, who had been drinking for ten years, trudged down the happy road of life. The road was long, seventy years long, but this was a happy alcoholic who loved life, loved to drink, and loved to love. At the ten-year

[9] Frank Lawless, *Not My Child: A Progressive and Proactive Approach for Healing Addicted Teenagers and Their Families* (Carlsbad, CA: Hay House, 2013), 20–21.

crossroad, the alcoholic was still feeling pretty good; even though the "ism" had set in, the alcoholic didn't know it, so life was good. The next crossroad would be at fifteen years. A crossroad consisted of two paths; one path was to continue to do what they were doing, and the other path consisted of the unknown. What the alcoholic didn't know was that down one crossroad, death and destruction lay in wait. As the alcoholic went to the twelve-year mark, he experienced some problems; the hangovers were getting worse. The alcoholic liked to sleep longer and longer, and he became lazier and lazier during the day. Oh, the alcoholic liked to play, but work was the problem. The alcoholic became more and more obsessed with alcohol; now, instead of drinking occasionally, they drank more often until the once-in-a-while habit became every day. At the fourteen-year mark, God asked the alcoholic how they were feeling.

The alcoholic said, tired. Nothing seems to go my way. I don't have any friends, and my finances are almost gone. I can't work or think like I used to when I was younger.

God said, what do you think the problem is?

The alcoholic answered, age, bad luck. And everyone I meet is the problem.

God informed the alcoholic that at any time they could turn down the unknown crossroad and end the drinking.

The alcoholic, being defiant, said no. The alcoholic made it to the fifteen-year crossroad and passed it up quickly, for now the alcoholic knew what was down his path: drinking alcohol daily and death.

As the alcoholic made it to the sixteenth-year mark, they noticed in a moment of clarity that he had nothing;

the family had left them, and the bank account was empty. They didn't have any nice clothes left and had no money to spend. All the money was now being spent on a little food and alcohol. Fifteen times the alcoholic had become sick with flu and stomach problems, not to mention the other physical problems. But the alcoholic was insistent on drinking whenever they wanted to, where they wanted to, and whatever they wanted to. The alcoholic was special and deserved this little peace of mind that alcohol provided each day, and the alcohol really gave them peace of mind now, to the point of blackouts.

The alcoholic never realized alcohol was the problem; everything else was the problem, including God, who didn't grant them good luck, fame, and fortune. Pretty soon a friend joined the alcoholic on the road. The alcoholic said, who are you?

The friend said, I am an angel sent by God to help you.

The alcoholic said, thank you; can you give me money?

The angel said no.

Can you give me food or fun? Maybe some clothes?

The angel said no.

The alcoholic, now getting angry and defiant, having met this angel, said, then there is nothing you can do for me.

The angel said, oh, but there is. I can give you hope. I can guide you down the road to an unknown good life.

The alcoholic replied, I don't need words. What I need is another good drink, another good party, another good fling, and money.

The angel said, okay, then the choice is yours, for I cannot help someone who won't help himself.

The alcoholic trudged on to the eighteen-year mark; now they had nothing—no clothes, no food, no kids, no family. They were always seeking someone to help, to give to them, to provide for them. The alcoholic was really becoming disturbed and angry. They started thinking about turning down the twenty-year unknown crossroad. By the nineteenth year, the person still couldn't figure out how to make their self better, to get money, to get food, to get a career, or to get dignity and respect. The alcoholic had an idea. They would beckon the angel and seek advice.

The angel appeared, and the alcoholic asked, how can I become a better person?

The angel replied, try praying to God daily. Ask him for the strength to overcome your drinking. The angel also replied, why don't you stop doing bad things to your body and do good things to yourself? Why don't you learn? Why don't you try to make good choices for yourself? Why don't you try to increase your income and then spend the money on good things, like more learning? Why don't you do something nice for somebody else instead of always asking someone to help you? It's always you and always about you. The angel said, take responsibility for all areas of your life, your welfare, and your well-being. Listen when God speaks to you. You always know right from wrong, and you have a choice every second of the day. If in that instant in time you decide you want a drink, you now have a choice to say no, rather than yes, because you now have that choice, that knowledge. You can now care about yourself. And you cannot care about anyone else until you care about yourself first.

The alcoholic was flabbergasted by this talk, by these words. By now their vocabulary was very limited because of all the brain cells they had killed, and they sometimes had a hard time communicating with other people. But they did know this: for the first time in their life, the alcoholic had a choice. Every second of the day and every day of the week, step by step the alcoholic became better without drinking.

Even when everyone else looked like he or she was having fun, now without alcohol, they could see the past, present, and future. With alcohol they could see only the past and present. For the first time, the alcoholic became aware that they had complete control of their thinking; their attitude, right and wrong, good and bad, everything became clearer and clearer each day. As the alcoholic became more aware of doing good and bad things to them self, they started seeking more and more good things for their self. It didn't take long for the alcoholic to be aware of good thinking and that self-pleasure was really self-destruction.

The alcoholic beckoned the angel, and said, good things are happening to me. How do I make them continue?

The angel said, you don't make anything continue. God does, and you have already answered your own question— that your job is to take care of yourself daily, make good choices, know when you are veering off the main path, know when you are doing something destructive to yourself, be in control of your life and your thinking, and take responsibility for yourself. You already know the right answer; all you have to do is practice it every second of the day, and then God will make things better. God makes things better. You make things worse.

As each year passed, the alcoholic could see clearer and clearer, and things did get better. At the twenty-fifth-year mark, the alcoholic beckoned the angel, and asked, how could I have been so stupid, so blind, so ignorant about using alcohol for all those years?

The angel replied, you were blinded by alcohol, by greed, lust, gluttony, anger, pride, sloth, and envy. You wanted to be happy; rather than bringing happiness, you wanted to be noticed with pride. Rather than being humble, you wanted to satisfy your lust. Rather than giving pleasure, you wanted to take instead of giving. You see you wanted all the wrong things. It is good to want a modest amount of each, but you wanted a lot, and the alcohol provided you with the desire to want more than your share of everything, so all your time was spent wanting.

The alcoholic said, sometimes I feel like another drink.

The angel said, go ahead, now you have a choice. You now know what lies down the path with alcohol, and you now know what lies down the path without alcohol. The path with alcohol will bring you instant gratification, and you will have no future. The path with no alcohol will bring you gratification for the rest of your life, a future, and humility, because good things will come to you if you work for it. If a person decides to take a step off the path and make a bad decision, then you will suffer. If a person stays on the path, good things will happen, and love will grow. If a person concentrates on himself or herself and does good things, then the benefits will flow to everyone.

At this point God appeared and said, my child, what have you learned in the last forty years?

And the alcoholic said humbly, I have learned choices and faith, everything I need to know to live a good life. I have learned to take care of myself, help others, and make good choices. I have learned to have faith, to accept the grace of God, and with that I have hope. I have learned to listen, follow directions, and allow God to work in my life with humility. I have learned everything I need to know to live a good life. With that I have peace of mind, and I am happy, joyous, and free. Amen. (Anonymous)

Here are some short affirmations on the benefits of recovery: "Wow," "Unbelievable," "A miracle," "I am so thankful," "I can't believe I ever got into alcoholism," "Recovery has been the greatest experience in my life," "Thank God," "I so wish I had gotten sober younger," and the list goes on and on. Recovery, a miracle in itself, may allow your spouse to come back to you, or your relationship now has a chance to get better. Family may come back to you. Finances will get better. Mental, physical, and spiritual health will all get better. You, the alcoholic, won't be alone anymore. Recovery is like a reinvention; the alcoholic now has the opportunity to start life over and become anything he or she wants. Goals and dreams will reappear. Accomplishments will happen. The alcoholic will experience life as he or she never experienced it before. Attitudes will change, people will treat him or her differently, and he or she will be better accepted. The alcoholic will now know how to solve life problems and will know how to live alcohol free. An air of what's positive will overtake the person's life. We are all in different levels of awareness in our lives; as the alcoholic recovers, he or she grows in self-awareness. As self-awareness increases, so do the opportunities and positive things in your life. What the alcoholic has experienced in recovery and will experience in the future can only be described as a miracle.

Chapter 5

Positive Living and Lifestyle Changes in Recovery

Anatomy of a Lifestyle Change

A lifestyle change is simply anything you are doing today that is different from what you were doing in the past. This is a broad area that encompasses many areas in life. The purpose of a lifestyle change should always be to enhance yourself, to make yourself better, and to be the best you can be. As you do so, things in life just get better and better. Don't underestimate yourself and your ability to bring goodness into your life or the world. Sometimes change requires risk, but if something isn't working in life, let go of it and try something new. Take care of yourself first. Once you have accomplished this, then you are ready to move forward. You can start with the five areas of life below.

There are five areas of life: career, family, spiritual area, psychological area, and physiological area. These are referred to as the "circle of life." When you spend time in each area, you will be in balance. All lifestyle changes can be categorized into one of the five areas of life. Some people spend time only in career and family most of their lives. When this happens, this person will be out of balance. The earlier a person can understand to make a concerted effort in the spiritual, psychological, and physiological areas, the sooner his or her life will become fulfilling, successful, rewarding, and balanced. It is this person who can stand alone with God and know he or she is truly doing good things in life.

Everyone is at different levels of awareness in his or her life. The basic level of self-awareness is fulfilling your basic needs for food, clothing, and shelter. A higher level of self-awareness would be educating yourself in as many areas as possible. The highest level of self-awareness is your progress at being the best you can be. Do you have the ability to now help other people or many other people? Can you initiate good life-changing or world-changing events for the betterment of mankind? The five areas of life are the basics of life, the foundation of life.

Five Areas of Life

Career

A career isn't a job; it's lifelong way of life. A career is what you choose to do every day for the rest of your life. A career must be productive work, something you have passion for, something you like and get satisfaction from each day. Anyone can get a job. A career must be made and strived for; it doesn't happen overnight. Find something you like and start doing it; find ways to perfect it and keep perfecting it, knowing it will never be perfect. This will be a lifetime job. A career will provide you with money for the betterment of your life. A job will usually provide for your basic needs. If you have a job, try to move your life toward a career. A career will have potential, opportunity for growth, and advancement.

Family

Almost everyone has a family in one form or another. If you are a parent, practice being a teacher to your kids about life for life. If you are a spouse, be a good one. Be a leader to the people around you. The best leaders lead by example. Teach others how to live, how to succeed; teach them morals, values, and beliefs. Living a good, positive lifestyle takes work. As you teach it, it does become easier, because you now practice what you preach. Practice being the best you can be every day, every hour, and good things will come. You cannot teach what you don't have.

If you don't have family, seek one out, in the form of groups, church groups, or positive-living groups. There is a group for almost everything, but you must seek them out. An example of a positive-living group may be a church family or an AA fellowship, any group or fellowship that helps keep a person focused on learning and living life in a positive manner. A positive-living group will be good for you, your friends, and your family. Generally, any religious or spiritual group may be in this category. Take care of your family and your spouse.

Spiritual

Spiritual training can come in a variety of forms, from praying or meditating to belonging and committing to a church. Many people find their spiritual growth by belonging to a church, much like a family. They are committed to learning, to supporting the church, its values, and its activities; and if you search, you will find one that is comfortable for you. Churches offer everything from weekly services, singles' groups, retreats, social groups, and study groups. They have many activities that will help you grow spiritually.

Prayer and meditation are more personal types of spiritual growth and can be done alone or in groups. They help you get in touch with your inner self, your higher power (whatever that may be), or God. Meditation sometimes comes in the form of positive-living groups, whose intent is the same as a church, to help you gain inner peace and awareness.

God is a Savior, and meditation is the path to God for knowing one's own self. A person can pick and choose a church, church activities, or a positive-living program; he or she can teach or preach meditation and choose to commit himself or herself to a spiritual relationship rather than learning a belief system. Learning and growing in this area will excel as long as a person remains independent of alcohol and is committed.

If you have little spiritual growth, you are probably functioning on self-will. Self-will doesn't always work, and how many times does a person need the help of a higher power, God, or the power of a group? There is also a direct correlation between faith and fear. The more fear you have, the less faith you will have; and the more faith you have, the less fear you will have. Spiritual growth will help you get peace of mind.

Psychological

This aspect of living comes in many forms. What you want to seek out is good mental health activities for yourself, learning, and doing positive healthy things. Pick any new activity, hobby, or field of study. When learning occurs, this is psychological growth. In terms of what's psychological, we are talking about having peace of mind, learning, seeing positive growth, and becoming a better person—finding more self-confidence, having better self-esteem, being more balanced, and embracing a thinking pattern that produces good results.

The psychological area can also mean a good lifestyle, spiritual growth, nutrition, or even a career that is good for you. It may mean good relationships and friends who support you in your decisions and efforts. The psychological area encompasses so many areas for the sole purpose of being content, healthy, and happy. Imagine doing good things constantly, accomplishing good things for yourself, striving for perfection, having a humble attitude, being a leader who is thankful and righteous in the biblical sense of the word, doing something good for others, and embracing a total sense of well-being. The psychological area simply means having good mental health, being the best you can be, and doing good things for others and yourself in all areas of your life.

Everyone has a mental and physical age. The longer alcoholics drink, the more they suppress their emotional and mental maturity for an equal amount of time. Thus, if alcoholics drink for twenty years, their mental maturity is somewhere back when they started drinking. There is a difference between mental age and maturity. With mental maturity, we gain wisdom, but alcohol stops or restricts mental maturity.

Physiological

The physiological area is your body's well-being, which includes nutrition, exercise, and the health of your body. Nutrition is your knowledge regarding good foods and what you eat. Exercise would be a key element of this area. The physiological area may mean do you get a health checkup on a regular basis? Are you learning how to take care of your body the best you can?

Balance

Spending time in each of the five areas will lead you to be in balance. When you achieve balance in your life, you will know it. It will give you such a sense of well-being, self-confidence, and peace of mind. At this level of awareness, you may achieve many great things. Leave one area out of your life or spend too little time in one area, and you will be out of balance. Specific areas of your life won't be right and will manifest problems in time.

When you spend your time in each of the five areas, you are said to be in balance. You have taken care of your mental health, physical health, spiritual health, career, and family. These areas give the ultimate feeling and purpose in life. You now have the strongest foundation to live and build on. Take a shortcut or leave one of the five areas out, and problems will manifest themselves. Being in balance is a place where a person can now move into what is referred to as self-actualization, the ability to now be the best person you can be. This is where a person is now ready to do things that can help many other people, or the person can become a good leader or change the world. This is the place where great things happen. Being in balance is the most satisfying place to be in life.

Examples

Here are some examples of lifestyle changes in each of the five areas of life. An improvement to the physiological area may mean having better nutrition, implementing a new and better exercise routine, giving up smoking, or having regular checkups with a physician. An improvement to any part of your health can be considered a lifestyle change. If you are a recovering alcoholic, seek out ways to improve your physical health and nutrition.

An improvement in the psychological area may equate to learning anything new, developing a new skill, experiencing new and different entertainment in your life (such as opera), or doing something you haven't tried before. This could be reading a self-help book on areas you may be weak on. How about learning to play the banjo or any instrument? Maybe you could learn a new way to improve your relationship with your spouse or children. How could you improve your friendships? Anything good for your mental state of mind could be considered a lifestyle change in this area. Remember, we all seek peace of mind, but how do we get there? If you're a recovering alcoholic, look for ways to improve your mental health. Counseling, going to meetings at Alcoholics Anonymous, attending church, reading, and learning are some ideas. Learning is a lifetime job.

If you seek a lifestyle change in the spiritual area, that can lead you into several different areas. If you aren't a person who goes to church, try it. Seek out a church and try it three times; if you like it, continue. If you don't like it, seek out a different church. A spiritual change might mean trying a Bible study group in your church or some church activities. Another option for the spiritual area is to learn to meditate or try yoga. These may be new or different to you, but if you like them, keep doing them; if not, seek something else. Maybe you just want to learn how to pray better; seek that out in a church or a book.

For the recovering alcoholic, all good things are tools to seek peace of mind.

In the area of a career, seek a career you like. If you're in a career you don't like, start taking the steps to find a different one. If you're in a job, seek a career. A career is a pursuit in which you spend most of your time in life; make it something you like.

If you are a recovering alcoholic, do you have a job or career? Seek the steps necessary to improve yourself. Write out an action plan, list the steps required to get there, and get into action. An action plan is just the steps you will take to get to where you want to be. If you want to be an air-conditioning technician, maybe the next step is to go to a city college for two years and get a technical degree. Now put the plan into action and enroll.

A family lifestyle change can be what you are going to do to improve your family or your relationship with your spouse, children, or relatives. Maybe you could take some classes on how to be a better parent or consider some counseling to improve being a spouse. You don't need to wait for a problem to arise before getting counseling; you can get counseling to prevent problems in the future. Have you ever asked your spouse, "How can I be a better spouse?" Try it, and the answer may surprise you. Many books on all topics are available.

If you're a recovering alcoholic, take a truthful look at your family and ask yourself how much damage you've done while drinking. Now, stop beating yourself up about it; you cannot change things from the past. What you can do is set out to repair the damage, starting now, and improve your family relationships. Seek counseling, meetings, readings—anything that will improve your relationship with your spouse and family. Seek out a mentor or sponsor, sometimes referred to as a life coach. You'll be surprised by how many people will help you if you ask. Many people will help you if you're helping yourself. A life coach, mentor, or sponsor will help guide you in your decisions and choices, and basically teach and guide you in life from their knowledge, experience, and wisdom.

If you are a spouse of a drinking person or an alcoholic, effort in these five areas will help you regain your self-esteem. It will allow you to find yourself again and start feeling good about yourself and your self-worth. The more and longer an alcoholic drinks, the more difficult this downward spiral will be for the drinker and the spouse. At each lower level of the spiral, the drinking person can turn it around at any time by stopping the alcohol. Otherwise the spiral goes lower and lower. This is a guaranteed fact of alcoholism. Once the spiral is reversed, life will go back up and get better. This is when we pray for a moment of clarity for the alcoholic, an intervention by God, to help him or her make the right choice to stop drinking.

These are some of the simplest forms of lifestyle changes, with a couple of examples in each. A lifestyle change encompasses so much more and is a broad spectrum in life. The purpose is to be the best you can be. Wake up every morning with energy and a zest for life, for improvement. Start with what you can improve today, whether it's a relationship with a spouse, finances, car maintenance, education, friends, or a job. What is it you can improve? This is all about progress and action, not perfection. A lifestyle change should be good for you.

Overview of a Lifestyle Change

A lifestyle change for a drinking person or alcoholic means adopting a nondrinking lifestyle, which means living one day at a time. A lifestyle change means an adjustment in the way one thinks, sometimes 180 degrees. It means doing healthy and good things, and liking yourself. It means getting out of yourself. This process has to do with living a life that is addiction free, helping others by using the knowledge you have gained, and continuing to live a good life for yourself, a healthy, good life where you feel good about yourself and the things you do. Be proud of what you do and who you are. Be thankful for the gift you have been given mentally, physically, and spiritually. You are now addiction free and have a choice of whether you do the addiction again.

Change can occur for several different reasons. Life difficulties can cause change. A strong desire can cause change, or hope can cause change. Change may be precipitated by fear—fear of the unknown, the reluctance to get out of one's comfort zone, the fear of losing something that is partially working. Or change can be a deliberate action on your part, a desire to change for the better.

Sometimes there is fear and risk when trying to make change. The point is that you have to think about things to make them better; then you must make a plan of action, a step-by-step process for how you're going to accomplish the change. It's the fear of change that keeps abusive relationships together because someone is fearful of the change to leave the abusive relationship (How will they live? How will they survive?). Or the abuser is fearful of changing his or her behavior because that would require learning, counseling, and even eliminating the alcohol. It's this fear of the unknown that stops people from achieving their dreams.

Change becomes a reality when you put a plan together and then actually put the plan into action. Change may be difficult in the beginning unless you have an action plan. The same is true for any goal. Put the idea down on paper and build on it, with a step-by-step process. Put the steps down on paper that are needed to achieve the change, then work each step. Once you have accomplished the steps, the change will have occurred. Build a good foundation for anything in life and then build on it.

A lifestyle change takes on new thinking and meaning for everything you do. Often people don't know exactly what it is they want, so they search for answers through church, seminars, schools, retreats, and books. When you hear the saying "Be the best you can be every hour of your life," grab on to it and start to practice it. Change may not happen quickly or overnight, but it must be worked at day by day, and in a few months or in time, you will know at some point that you have achieved your goal. You will know and feel the greatness life has to offer.

Positive lifestyle change can occur if people are conscious of it and want to change. Most people have some idea that they want more money or a bigger house. They'll diet, or they want a better job, but these desires are sometimes more about wanting than doing. The best suggestion I can give is to decide on the change you want to make; look at the end result. Where do you want to be in three months or a year? Then take the necessary steps, one at a time, to achieve that change. You also need to take a more in-depth look at the goal. Don't say, "I simply want to lose weight." Say, "I want to lose weight, and this is how I will do it step by step." Write down the steps needed to lose weight. I have seen weight-loss gurus use a step method in their weight-loss program, and their program is very successful if a person follows the steps. The same is true for the alcoholic using AA's twelve-step program. The same holds true for any positive change you want to make step by step.

There are some excellent lifestyle-change books on the market, including *Natural Medicine, Vitamins, Minerals, and Herbs* by Dr. Gary Null. Another is *Prescription for Nutritional Healing* by Phyllis Balch and Dr. James Balch. These books are worth a hundred times more than their cost due to their life-giving information; they will provide you with better health. Both authors have the most thoroughly informative books on nutrition and attitude, lifestyle changes, sickness prevention, and living a healthy life. If you think health is expensive and time consuming, it is not half as expensive and time consuming as sickness. It was a wise person who said, "It takes a very good person to take an interest in their own health."

People who consider themselves to be happy are happy to a degree. All people are at different levels of awareness or happiness at different times in their lives. Most people maintain slight improvements or more awareness as time goes on, but only those who seek out new and better methods—a new kind of thinking and more learning, can change their lives tremendously. If you make a deliberate, concerted effort to change, you can. If a person is happily married, happy with his or her job, living in his or her happy house, and doing the same good things day in and day out, I can guarantee you that this person is living at a higher awareness level.

The best change comes from within. This sentence is imperative to the alcoholic. An alcoholic must decide within himself or herself to stop drinking. If people make their own choice, they are more likely to keep it, compared to someone coerced into a change. It's so important for alcoholics to make their own choice to stop drinking.

If you are a recovering alcoholic, the lifestyle change will start with your sobriety date. Some changes will occur naturally without much thought.

For example, your body will start to heal itself after years of pouring alcohol into it. It is a slow process and will take approximately three months, though the complete process may take years. The cravings may last weeks or months, but at some point, they will pass, going away as subtly as they came. No alcoholic can ever tell you exactly when the cravings left. Once in a while, you may experience a craving for alcohol. Now you have new tools to use, and the key is how you act on the cravings.

Lifestyle changes can sometimes cause people to change individually or together in relationships. If someone in a relationship stops drinking, couples must be willing to relearn how to live. Lives and marriages can be reinvented or relearned into positive ones. If two people are willing to change, marriages will work if both are honest and want them to work. One of the most positive programs I have seen for couples can be found in counseling offered by churches or religious organizations. They have a plan, a method of counseling that provides the positive reinforcement and support that goes with a couple's success. It is a plan for a positive Christian marriage and lifestyle. It is all a matter of learning, awareness, and a desire to make it work. Life, living, and relationships all require some work. A relationship can be the best thing in life.

Learning

Trying new things can be part of learning. Contemplate what it is you need to learn and go learn it. Seminars, college classes, or night classes are some of the avenues to learn from. Learning from a mentor or a book can also help train you in a chosen field or skill, or it can broaden your knowledge on any given subject. Learning can be the greatest experience of your life. Learning is a lifelong job and must be sought out. Many people think learning stops with a high school or college diploma. Life is continually changing, and people are changing, too. Learning helps facilitate life so you can overcome obstacles, roadblocks, and setbacks. Learning and knowledge offer the answers to all our problems.

A positive life continues to learn. Those who don't learn will find themselves way behind the times of a normal society. Whether you are making lifestyle changes or working on your first days of sobriety, you will be learning. Both require two qualities to be successful: an open mind and a willingness to learn. Without these, nothing can happen, and your life will stay just as it always was.

If you are a recovering alcoholic or the spouse, if you keep practicing what you have learned, you will start feeling yourself coming into balance. Maintain humility always. Thank God for the knowledge you have been given and understand you have just experienced a miracle.

Lifestyle changes can take on many aspects. Make improvements to your morals, values, beliefs, and the five areas in life. When you build a basic, strong foundation, you can build on it, and the foundation will support all the good things you do or add to it. More miracles will come if you work for them.

Chapter 6

Alcoholism in the Family

If there is an alcoholic in the household, the disease becomes a family disease. The other family members didn't ask to get the disease; they just get it by association, sort of like the flu. When one member of the family gets the flu, no matter how hard other family members try not to get it, they end up with it anyway, just by being in the same household as the person with the flu. Likewise, with alcoholism, other family members become infected with the disease just by being in the same household. Even though a person doesn't drink, he or she becomes afflicted in the mind and spirit just by being around an alcoholic.

If you are the spouse of an alcoholic, you will be the one most affected. The nondrinking spouse will be affected mentally, spiritually, financially, socially, or physically. Your self-esteem may disappear. At some point in the relationship, a nondrinking spouse may have to make the ultimate choice of staying with the alcoholic and functioning as an individual in the relationship or leaving the alcoholic and functioning as a single person. Households become dysfunctional, emotions and feelings are distorted daily, and alcohol is a constant drain on the finances. In many instances, the nondrinking spouse becomes the enabler by allowing the alcoholic to spend money on alcohol and to drink. Due to today's awareness level, everyone is now aware of spousal abuse and domestic violence. To the nondrinking spouse, this chapter and this book are also written for you.

Being around an alcoholic isn't usually a fun or positive experience. If you have one drinking parent or family member, other family members must compensate for the drinker's negative attitude. And over the years, particularly for a child while growing up, the drinking attitude and behavior take their toll on all other family members. While growing up, a child learns from the parents, and if one parent is a drinker, the child learns to cope later in life by drinking. Kids are like sponges; they soak up everything around them and are constantly learning so they can become independent, functioning members of society as adults. Those characteristics that may be consistent in alcoholics—excess pride, greed, lust, envy, sloth, anger, self-centeredness, negativity, the feel-sorry-for-me attitude, reactions, or fears—are usually passed on to the children. Compare those characteristics to a parent who walks in faith, humility, and gratitude, a parent who is a good leader; this is a parent who discusses rather than reacts, is thankful for everything instead of wanting more of everything, has faith in God, and practices a religious or spiritual life, or is positive, fun, and nice to be around. That is the difference for a child or spouse of an alcoholic.

Alcoholics tend to have depressed personalities anyway, and these feelings get worse when alcohol is added, because alcohol is a deliberate depressant. For someone who is already slightly depressed, add in some more depressant, and what do you get? A really depressed personality. This becomes a vicious cycle for the drinking person. This is where children and spouses become victims of the alcoholic because the depression may be subtle or it may be extreme, but it usually happens every time the person drinks.

Alcoholics have notorious reputations for being liars, thieves, and controllers; they seldom say what they mean or do what they say. Because alcohol is the priority in their lives, everything else becomes secondary, including children, spouses, work, and spiritual practice. Lying may become an acceptable survival tool to drinking people—having to lie about how much money is being spent or about the places or length of time they are drinking. Drinking people seldom remember commitments they made while drinking, thus making excuses to cover up what they didn't get done.

There are two theories regarding alcoholism; one is that it's a chemical imbalance in the brain that causes drinking, and the other is that it's a learned behavior. When alcohol is the subtle priority in one's life, this is what children learn. The reasons for drinking, having mental turmoil, and justifying drinking are practiced every time a person drinks. This is what children learn. If an alcoholic tells one lie, steals one thing, or isn't truthful in day-to-day dealings, this behavior is what children and spouses learn. Alcoholics are notorious for making a commitment and then not keeping it. They seldom say what they mean and mean what they say. People are generally grown up when they marry, so they have some sense of right and wrong. But how many times does a person marry someone who drinks too much? Then the spouse becomes part of the problem by not making good choices. The spouse thinks it will get better, but it seldom does.

No one with a normal amount of self-esteem and awareness would marry someone consistently drinking alcohol.

In the home, if a spouse says little about the alcoholic's drinking, he or she becomes the enabler. The alcoholic becomes dependent on that spouse's action of saying nothing about the drinking. So the situation is comfortable to the alcoholic but not to the spouse. If the spouse takes issue with the drinking, the situation usually becomes uncomfortable and confrontational, so a spouse may choose to keep quiet. This type of relationship is referred to as a "dependent relationship."

Alcoholic families are dysfunctional. *Dysfunction* is defined as normal daily activities, relationships, and discussions not done in a productive way. *Normal* means positive, productive, and progressive. There are certain characteristics of dysfunctional relationships; one family member has to be the sick one, one member has to be the controller, one member has to be the jokester, or one member or more has to be dependent. Dysfunction in relationships, discussions, and normal daily activities aren't positive, progressive, or productive. The characteristics of an alcoholic may include having a low self-esteem or self-centered; all the characteristics feed into the dysfunctional family relationships. The family members develop behaviors to compensate for this type of behavior and environment. I'm always reminded of one saying. "Stay away from negative people, negative places, and negative things."

Family members of an alcoholic are constantly in the same house with a negative, drinking person. Because of this fact, family members develop fear behaviors that compensate for the unpredictable alcoholic and the effects the alcohol has on him or her in terms of self-esteem and how he or she handles daily life activities and decisions. Often a nondrinking adult child of an alcoholic will go on to marry an alcoholic, because this personality is perceived as normal to him or her.

Being a child around an alcoholic can have lifelong negative effects on him or her as an adult. He or she may have some or many of the same character defects present in the alcoholic. These defects begin to appear in the person's teen years or when he or she becomes a young adult. If these defects aren't corrected, they will be carried for a lifetime. Children learn daily from the people around them. As they reach their teen years and start practicing self-will, the character defects will start to manifest. This can be seen many times in problem teens.

Nondrinking adult children of alcoholics will benefit greatly from reading chapters 3 and 4 of this book. Once adults have accepted and acknowledged that they have these same characteristics as an alcoholic and why, they can begin to correct them. Once they develop a manner of living that demands rigorous honesty, then adult children can begin to heal themselves. Alcoholic parent(s) increasingly neglect their children's spiritual, physical, and mental growth and needs.

Alcohol in the family is a major contributor to divorce. In 2017, when divorce seems to be the norm and awareness of alcohol is higher than ever, just a little too much alcohol in the family may cause the family unit to break apart and end up in divorce. I can't stress enough that alcohol is a major contributor to spousal abuse, both mentally and physically, and domestic violence.

Alcohol in the family causes a type of behavior that isn't helpful to the progress or well-being of the family. First is the amount of money spent on alcohol. This alone will cause friction in families. When families need necessities, such as clothes, food, and shelter, the basics, and a portion of the money is wasted on alcohol or a good time for one person, spouses don't take well to this type of self-centered, wasted spending. And then if it is done again and again, spouses will react. If a young family has enough money to spend on alcohol, then it runs into another type of problem: the amount of time spent drinking, a self-centered selfish act for one person, the drinking person. A husband's job in a relationship is to take care of his wife's needs and vice versa. When the alcoholic spends a good deal of time on self-pleasure, this imbalance causes resentment not only from the nondrinking person but also from the children. In a family, depending on how often an alcoholic drinks, this is the way alcohol works; in the beginning, someone may consume one or two drinks to relax, but at some point this pattern changes to three or four or more drinks. That's the progression of the alcoholic disease.

Here is an actual alcohol-related family story. My wife and I went to a fine French restaurant, a very fancy place with escargot on the menu and other fine French dishes. She started ordering; luckily she knows French. There was a large family gathering a few tables over; it looked like three or four generations of family—grandparents, parents, adult kids, and small kids. The adults were drinking wine with their meal, and I noticed that the waitress frequently kept going back to the table; the more I watched, the more wine they ordered. After a while, they seemed to consume their wine quickly—in fact, large carafes of it.

This was a family social gathering; they seemed to be celebrating something, but most of the adults drank wine as fast as they could, just gulping it down. There is a glamorous world out there of wine connoisseurs, who smell and sip wine for its fine qualities. I didn't see any connoisseurs at that table. As the meal progressed, apparently the five-star meal was secondary to the family, and drinking wine seemed to be their primary purpose for being there. It didn't seem that these people were drinking wine for its fine taste or qualities; they were drinking it for the alcohol.

Do you ever notice people who buy large quantities of alcohol, cases and cases of wine or alcohol? This may be a big red flag for a problem with alcohol. Your nationality or economic status doesn't matter when you buy cases and cases of liquor or wine. Whether you drive a Mercedes and have money or don't have money doesn't matter. When you drink to excess for the effect of the alcohol, this is referred to as a drinking problem. Alcoholism does not discriminate.

This fine family now became loud and boisterous, and the poor waitress kept going over there every ten minutes to bring more wine. In reality what these adults were doing was teaching each younger generation at the table to consume alcohol in the name of family, fun, and celebration, and this is the way we celebrate. The younger people at the table will learn it's okay to drink, because it's fine wine, a fine family, and a fine celebration. They can't wait to be twenty-one because of how much fun it must be, with all the adults laughing, being loud, drinking, and getting the "glow." Believe it or not, you can have an equal amount of fun without alcohol.

The moral to this story is that alcohol is subtle; when the family dispersed and went back to their normal lives, which ones consume excessive amounts of wine at home? Which people went on to be alcoholics? This is the disease of alcoholism in full bloom. This is how alcoholism is passed from generation to generation. Little kids, like little sponges, soak up all this information, and when they try their first glass of wine, their first little glow occurs. This is the subtle disease of alcoholism taking hold in full bloom and flourishing; it is passed from parent to child.

There is a lot of information about the health benefits of a glass of wine a day; it lowers cholesterol, dissolves plaque, is good for the heart, and reduces heart attacks. I believe that drinking a glass of wine a day does have beneficial effects on the body and heart, but alcoholics and many wine drinkers don't partake of only one glass a day. Many wine drinkers have lost the ability to drink only one glass a day. When they consume wine, they consume multiple glasses or large volumes. These people have let the potential for alcoholism set in, and they are no longer drinking for the health benefits; they are drinking for the effects of the alcohol. Many wine drinkers like alcoholics justify their actions and have lost that prestigious ability to be wine connoisseurs.

Parents: Identifying a Young Person's Alcohol Use

This section is for parents and offers some tips for identifying whether a young person is using alcohol. Many of the characteristics identified in the section on adult children of alcoholics will be similar.

The characteristics of a young person using alcohol will be similar to those of an adult. One main clue is a fake ID. Fake IDs are used for only two reasons: buying alcohol and getting into a club where alcohol is served. Other clues may be stealing money, being listless and defiant, having a self-willed attitude, doing whatever they want to do, feeling unwell in the mornings, having hangovers, or oversleeping. Keep in mind that young people are going through mental, physical, hormonal, and social changes that can cause many of the same behaviors.

Parents, watch your children when they come home at night; one of the best ways to identify drinking is by checking smell, speech, or behavior. Slurring words, staggering, stumbling, and being unable to focus are all signs of alcohol use. If you believe your young person is drinking, seek counseling immediately. Open a positive and progressive conversation with your young person and talk about why he or she feels the need to try alcohol. Also discuss consequences of drinking, peer pressure, choices, self-esteem, and the need to say no. Talk about many of the sub-titles in this book and seek counseling.

If you need a more hard-core approach, take your young person to a homeless encampment and socialize for a while so they can see the consequences of alcohol. Usually you won't be welcome in an alcohol treatment center, but bring your young person to an Alcoholics Anonymous meeting; you are welcome as a visitor. Sit in the meeting as a visitor and listen to the stories associated with the consequences of alcohol. Seek out a speaker meeting in AA; you can learn a lot. The Salvation Army usually has at least one weekly speaker or panel meetings on alcohol, which are very informative; visitors are welcome. AA has a young person's meeting, called Alateen, where a teen can learn. Alateen has meetings, speakers, and nondrinking social events. Alateen has to be sought out since such meetings aren't in every city. If you are a parent, the worst thing you can do is nothing. Help your young person raise his or her self-esteem and self-awareness level, value, and self-worth.

Here is an alcohol-related story based on alcohol in the family. Three related ladies were at a club, one of whom was twenty years old. The twenty-year-old was somehow also drinking and drove home. She nodded off and rolled the van on its side on the freeway at night. A bus hit the van while going sixty-five miles per hour. Two ladies were killed, but the twenty-year-old driver survived.

This is another example of the incomprehensible demoralization of alcohol in the family.

Alcoholism is a family disease, and when there is one drinker in the household, the whole family is affected. In one form or another, one attitude or another, one character defect or another, the disease spreads to all members. A spouse who stays with a consistent drinker becomes involved in the sickness and tries to cope with the episodes. The spouse waits for things to become normal again. The problem with this thinking is that episodes become more frequent, and they last longer and longer until soon the nondrinking spouse is living with an alcoholic who is taking the family downhill one inch at a time financially, morally, mentally, physically, or spiritually. If both spouses have a problem with alcohol, the problems are multiplied by ten, and everything is out of control.

There is a fine line between normal drinking and alcoholic drinking. The disease is so subtle that the nondrinking spouse keeps thinking it's going to get better, and maybe sometimes it does, but at some point in time, it gets worse, and slowly, over many years or even decades, it never gets better.

Here is a paradox regarding many young people. They may not especially be practicing good nutrition as young healthy adults, and with the need to fit in socially, they start out in life by going to parties where alcohol is present, and to be socially accepted they have a few drinks, and this event starts the alcohol cycle. Young adults' social lives may become more important than their health. Most young people are very focused on studying for a goal, fitting in social settings, finding themselves, experimenting with life, discovering who they are, and finding a spouse or mate. Nutrition may be low on their priorities list during this time. For young people, life is work and play; and soon thereafter, it may be the seeking of social activities, with nutrition still low on the priority list.

So here you have a young person, low on the nutritional scale, and drinking alcohol occasionally. Alcohol provides what every human being desires: peace of mind and acceptance. Once young people or any person, for that matter, begins to use alcohol to feel good, he or she may soon forget that food is feel-good nutrition, and he or she may start substituting alcohol more often.

If you go back to the point in young persons' early lives, when they were experimenting with alcohol, if they had the awareness that alcohol was destructive and were conscious of nutrition and vitamins, the nutrition may have won over. Vitamins have no side effects; you feel good the next day, and your life spirals upward, with an occasional down, unlike alcohol. There are many things not taught in schools, and in the first twelve years, you probably learn only the five basic food groups. Maybe you learn a little more in high school, with maybe a mention of vitamins or that the American diet lacks nutrition and is filled with fats guaranteed to give you problems later in life. All alcoholics drink to achieve the glow, that state of mind in which everything is perfect without problems. They also get peace of mind, pleasure, and goodness; and they feel so good and warm and fuzzy. The glow is that ultimate level of fantasy; many great and not-so-great thoughts are achieved at this level. This level is short lived but may be obtained each night or each time the person drinks.

When you talk with alcoholics, they will all tell you that it's the glow that is continually strived for with alcohol. Yes, there are a million reasons for drinking, but the glow is the ultimate reason. If only alcoholics knew how to meditate, would they understand at this point that the same feeling can be achieved with meditation. After the "ism" has set in for alcoholics, they have no more choices about drinking. Once they make the choice not to drink again, they now have choices again.

Intervention

Interventions have been around for some time, known to the alcoholic community. Intervention is sometimes a tool to be used as a last resort for recovery. Never give up hope on the alcoholic. Sometimes in one day, a hard-core, long-term, extreme alcoholic has a change of heart and wants to stop drinking. This is sometimes referred to as a moment of clarity or the grace of God. In the past year, the word *intervention* has become more well known because of social media. Theoretically an intervention is the process in which family members gather, tell the alcoholic how much they love him or her, and give the alcoholic an ultimatum to go to treatment; otherwise, all ties, food, shelter, clothing, and money will stop.

Only experienced interventionists should do an intervention. These people know and understand alcoholism. Don't take an intervention lightly, because there can be dire consequences. Interventions are usually reserved for extreme alcoholics, sometimes referred to as "low bottom" alcoholics. These people may be living in substandard living conditions, or their lives drastically take a nosedive because of alcohol. Many may be fairly close to death at this stage.

On the other hand, many alcoholics are fairly independent, have some sort of income, and aren't dependent on anyone for anything. These types of people may be more reluctant to do treatment. Deep down in every hard-core alcoholic's heart, there is that one hopeful spot of not drinking. This is the spot you try to find and build on. Never give up on the alcoholic and pray and hope that God will intervene. Intervention is a tool, and if the alcoholic agrees to go to treatment, the family steps up to support this change and recovery. At this stage, family members may also need counseling because they may have become as affected by alcoholism as the alcoholic. All the family members need to learn a new nondrinking lifestyle in the way they communicate, interact, and handle life. An intervention can be a successful tool to get the alcoholic to go to treatment.

Family Recovery

If the alcoholic recovers from alcoholism, there is a lot of repair work to be done with the family. While the alcoholic should be doing some counseling or working through a positive-living program. There are programs for the spouse. Alanon is for the nondrinking spouse, and Alateen is for the young person in an alcoholic household. The whole family can learn the same recovery tools and living program as the alcoholic.

If you are the nondrinking spouse, most of the subtitles in this book are also intended for recovery for you. Read them, practice them, and seek out meetings of Alanon or some other counseling or positive-living program. Alanon has one of the most appropriate sayings. "Detach with love." Alanon will teach how to help and how not to help the alcoholic. But most important, it will teach you how to help yourself, rebuild your self-esteem, and show how not to be an enabler; and it will teach you how to get "you" back again. It will reteach you to be a whole, good, independent person again. There are so many life benefits of living in an alcohol-free home; don't give up hope.

Pregnancy

Also, please take a special imperative note that alcohol is devastating for the fetus of a pregnant mother. Pregnant mothers should avoid all alcohol. Drinking alcohol while pregnant is highly likely to produce *fetal alcohol syndrome*, in which the newborn baby may be mentally retarded to varying degrees. Once alcohol is consumed, brain development in the unborn baby is distorted or interrupted. I cannot stress and pray enough for all pregnant mothers; don't consume alcohol while pregnant. This may be the most important paragraph in this book, and I cannot stress enough the importance of not drinking while pregnant.

Cost of Alcoholism

The cost of alcoholism is incomprehensible. If you spend $5 a week on alcohol, the cost is $260 a year or $2,600 for ten years. If you spend $5 a day on alcohol, then the cost is $1,825 a year or $18,250 for ten years. Now we're talking some significant dollars, and for thirty years it would be $54,750. For a daily drinker who may be spending $10 a day on alcohol, the bill for a year would be $3,650 and $36,500 for ten years. For thirty years, it would be $109,500, a significant amount.

Add in the cost for doctors' visits because of physical ailments or an alcohol treatment facility; the cost can be $1,500 to $3,000 a day, and a normal stay is fifteen days. That is a minimum of $22,500 for treatment. Some stays can normally go thirty to ninety days. Or add in some professional counseling at $100 to $150 per hour at a minimum of ten hours; that equates to a minimum of $1,000 to $1,500. The normal counseling time can be one hour every week for six to twelve months. Once-a-week counseling for a year will cost a minimum of $5,200 to $7,800. So that $7.99 bottle of liquor on sale isn't so cheap.

Oh, also don't forget to add in the family members and their cost for counseling, so whichever formula or cost you are using, just double or triple that amount to get your family members back to normal. For extras, you can add in any cost of alcohol-related diseases that require hospitalization or surgery. Now I think I have covered all the consequential costs of that one bottle of $7.99 liquor on sale. Maybe not. Add in the cost of divorce, child support, and/or alimony, and any other related costs to alcoholism. So, for the $7.99 bottle of liquor on sale, the consequential cost could be approximately $250,000, plus the potential of losing one's job and all income. The bottom line—and I'll say it again—is that the cost of alcoholism is incomprehensible.

Adult Children of Alcoholics

This section is devoted to the adult children of alcoholics. It's important for adult children to recognize some of the characteristics they learned while growing up with an alcoholic parent. With a little help or counseling, they can recognize and correct these deficiencies.

Children who grew up with a functioning alcoholic learn and develop some of the character defects the drinking parent has. Grown-up children of alcoholics can be like a dry drunk, a person who stops drinking but doesn't learn anything new. These alcoholics have the same negative personality they did while drinking. An adult child may not be as extreme as a drinking person; they may have some of the characteristics of a drinker in thinking and attitude.

Keep in mind that there are two types of children of alcoholics, those who don't drink and those who do. Those who drink grow up and become like their parents. Those who don't drink grow up and may possess some of the personality traits and attitudes their drinking parent had. As people grow up, they develop life skills, including how to cope with life. People normally will keep what works and change what doesn't. Children of alcoholics have been given a distorted set of morals, values, and beliefs—or none at all.

Grown-up children have some of the same thinking alcoholics have; they are great reactors. They grew up with a parent who reacted constantly to everything instead of having proactive, progressive discussions. This is how children learned to behave as adults; if they react the loudest and hardest, a technique they learned as a child, they may get their way.

Adult children of alcoholics could well develop one or more of the following characteristics to some varying degree:

- Being controlling or manipulative
- Lying, stealing, or making excuses
- Having excessive lust or gluttony
- Tending to negativity, having depression, being unaware of feelings
- Not being thankful or giving
- Being reactionary or resentful
- Having low self-esteem, shyness, or oversensitivity
- Harboring guilt, anger, fear, or shame

- Being loud or boisterous
- Exhibiting "big shotism" or pride
- Showing excess greed or envy
- Being self-centered or isolated
- Living like an overachiever or workaholic

Children of alcoholics have learned by a certain age that they are a little different from everybody else. They may have some of the same feelings as an alcoholic; they never quite feel like they fit in. They feel like they are different.

An adult child of an alcoholic may overreact to everything. Everything is like a personal attack on them; they may overcompensate by becoming extremely loud and boisterous. Max Ehrman (1872–1945), a great American writer, once wrote, "Avoid loud and boisterous people, for they are a vexation to the spirit."

We have all seen and been around loud, boisterous, and braggart people. They are extremely hard to be around, with that constant bragging about themselves—what they have, how good they are, why they are the best of everything. This is an overcompensation for low self-esteem. No one else in life ever told them how good they are or gave them compliments, so they give themselves compliments. These adult children may be overly self-centered.

Another compensation method for an adult child of an alcoholic is possibly being oversensitive, because of the constant negativity directed toward them as children, including the regular put-downs, the perpetual feeling of never being good enough, and the lack of praise. Children learn by guidance, limits, boundaries, and trial and error. When guidance is too much or the limits and boundaries are too narrow or too wide, certain negative behaviors start to take place. A good leader leads by example. When the leader of the family is a controller, he or she tries to control a child verbally or physically to an extreme degree. When the limits and boundaries are too narrow, the child reacts with defiance. When the boundaries are too wide, the child develops a manner of living in which he or she can do whatever he or she wants, and there is a lack of self-discipline.

Nondrinking adult children of alcoholics will often benefit greatly from practicing a twelve-step program. There are anonymous meetings titled just that: "Adult Children of Alcoholics." These meetings will provide the person with a positive program for living. This program will allow the nondrinking adult child to correct his or her current alcoholic type of thinking or behavior that was learned while growing up.

Children of alcoholics are the real victims, because they never had a chance to learn a good, right, and positive way of living. At least with the drinking adult, his or her behavior can be blamed on the alcohol, but the adult child of an alcoholic doesn't have that excuse.

Nondrinking adult children of alcoholics will benefit greatly from reading chapters 1 and 2. Once adult children have accepted and acknowledged that they have learned these same characteristics as an alcoholic and why, they can now begin to correct them. Once they develop a manner of living that demands honesty, adult children can begin to heal themselves. You cannot fix what you don't acknowledge.

If you are an adult child of an alcoholic, seek counseling. Find and attend meetings in your city for adult children of alcoholics, and your life will improve. You will then better understand some of the emotions and feeling you were taught growing up. These meetings will teach you how to live and love yourself; they will bring back your self-esteem and give you choices.

Chapter 7

Alcoholism in the Workplace

The purpose of this chapter is to give managers or employers an awareness of alcoholism in the workplace and discuss the role of managers in dealing with employees. This chapter is written for the small business owner or manager in a large organization or corporation.

The key expectations for any employee are performance, results, and attitude.

Any addiction in the workplace has the same general impact, whether it is alcohol, drugs, sex, gambling, or food. Even the adult child of an alcoholic may have some impact in the workplace; see the chapter on alcoholism in the family. In general, addiction in the workplace causes less efficiency, lowered profit, and additional employee problems.

Based on statistics, a large percentage of the general population engages in alcohol use at some time. A certain percentage of employees in a workplace may engage in some form of consistent alcohol use, depending on the workplace. Any percentage will result in lowered profits, and if the percentage goes higher, a business may find itself in jeopardy of bankruptcy.

As a manager, you cannot fix a drinking employee. If alcohol is causing a problem, then alcohol *is* the problem. Alcoholism in the workplace may be subtle and destructive, and it may not even be noticeable for years.

Alcoholism is in every walk of life and at the job place or site, and it may be at every level in an organization. If you work in a pyramid-type organization, alcohol can be at any level in the organization. Alcoholics are also at every financial level. They may have a tendency to be workaholics, or they may be lower producers. They usually are focused on their jobs and their drinking.

Alcoholism is subtle and progressive. It is socially acceptable, even in some workplaces. If a person has two drinks at lunch, by three o'clock he or she may have passed the alcohol, but the mind won't be fully functioning.

In the workplace, if the employer says nothing about poor work performance based on some type of expectations, the employer may unknowingly become the enabler. In the workplace, alcoholics become dependent on the employer to provide the dollars they need to support their habit. The employer can take issue with alcohol only if it is on the workplace premises or if the employee is drinking or drunk during work hours. The employer has no legal right in dealing with the issue of alcohol with the employee other than his or her job performance. If the employer takes issue with the alcohol, the employee will usually go into denial or have a multitude of excuses. If an employee denies alcohol use, there is nothing the employer can do, unless the employee is stumbling, being obnoxious, acting belligerent, falling down, causing safety issues, or inflicting some physical damage. Managers can legally deal only with performance or attitude issues that occur during working hours. Some businesses have a formal policy in place that defines inside and outside work behavior, including what is and what isn't acceptable.

Alcoholic Personalities in the Workplace

In the workplace, you may have two types of alcoholic personalities. The first type might be a quiet person, a hard worker who minds his or her own business and keeps the act of drinking private. The other type is the loud, boisterous person who may have a bad case of "big shotism" and doesn't hide his or her alcohol use at all. Usually, this person is the first to want to go out to lunch, especially for drinks. This type of employee is usually the most fun to be around because he or she is the life of the party. This may be a happy, funny person, and he or she is usually a good enough worker to get by using his or her personality and sociability skills. Sometimes these types are very popular because they are natural leaders, but they aren't good for the long haul. In the beginning or within a few years, these heavy drinkers experience problems, sometimes sexual, offensive, dishonest, careless job performance issues or physical ailments.

Characteristics of Alcoholism in the Workplace

- Tardiness is usually repetitious, and employees always have the best excuses for being late.
- Days off are frequent, and too many days are taken off, again for the best of reasons. Mondays are frequent days off for a drinker. Family issues are a very effective excuse because of the feel-sorry-for-me attitude, and no manager wants to question anybody very much about family issues, because of the strong emotions related to it.
- Drinkers are usually unpredictable. This issue comes under the subtitle of reacting. Sometimes they are happy, and in an instant, they are sad, mad, or angry. The manager doesn't even know what he or she did to cause it. The employees may be agreeable one minute and disagreeable the next, and they may react with great emphasis or emotion.
- Reacting is one of the key characteristics of many alcoholics; they overreact to anything. Alcoholics take so many things out of context. With a sharp tongue, they can verbally put someone down in an instant and attack his or her very nature. They take everything personally and are never able to let comments go by. Sometimes they will react with anger, sometimes with "big shotism," sometimes verbally, and sometimes physically. They are generally unthankful and don't like to listen or be told anything. Alcoholics may be argumentative, confrontational, and defiant. They despise being controlled, and they will argue any issue or nonissue. Alcoholics work best by suggestion.
- The focus and attention span of drinkers are generally very short; they may be very nervous and move around a lot; they may appear to be high strung or overly slow. Some of their short attention span

is attributed to physical problems, because if a person has drunk the night before, the body is constantly trying to rid itself of the toxin and what the stomach perceives to be an irritant. Gastritis is a common symptom of drinking.

- Alcoholics are pleasure seekers in any form or manner. They may be self-seeking, self-centered individuals, with an extreme, exaggerated sense of fun and pleasure, always trying to get others to drink with them.

- "Out to lunch" is an appropriate expression, since alcoholics have short attention spans. They may be out to lunch in more ways than one, sometimes literally, because with lunch comes a drink or a few. It is their opportunity to satisfy the addiction, and thirty minutes or an hour is never enough. Alcoholics will justify many reasons for going out to lunch, because this is social or business time where alcohol can be consumed, and it is socially acceptable. With this practice come excuses to leave early; the sooner they leave, the quicker they can start satisfying the addiction.

- Alcoholics will always seek out friends, people like themselves who drink. Seeking friendship is pretty normal with many people. Alcoholics will seek out only people who will socialize and drink with them.

Alcoholics are victim thinkers; anything that goes wrong is someone else's fault. Until drinkers enter an alcohol program, they are convinced that someone or something else—bad luck, a parent, a spouse, or the job—is causing their drinking. They have a million reasons to drink. What never enters their minds is that they are the cause of their drinking. Failure of tasks or responsibilities will always be attributable to someone else's failure. It is always someone else's fault.

Alcoholics are often perceived as liars, controllers, or manipulators. Because alcoholics are never sure who they really are, they never have consistent thinking patterns. When it comes to morals, values, and beliefs, they generally may not have any pertaining to themselves. They will have lots of opinions about other people, places, and things but none about themselves and what they stand for; this is referred to as integrity or the lack thereof.

They have learned to change their minds a lot to survive, and they will do or say whatever it takes to satisfy the addiction or to please others. Because of memory problems and their hidden agenda to drink, they will tell you one thing and change it four hours later, especially if there is a drinking episode in between. Many alcoholics frequently don't remember what they said yesterday. When it comes to commitments, the same is true. They may commit to doing something today and tomorrow won't even remember making the commitment, let alone what it was. In the workplace, this may be perceived as being untruthful or making excuses as to why something didn't get done.

Pride, greed, lust, envy, gluttony, anger, and sloth are known as the seven sins. Alcoholics will possess one or more of these to an extreme. Everyone may have some normal amount of each; the difference is that alcoholics will have an extreme amount in one or more. Anytime you have an extreme amount of any of these, balance and harmony won't be achieved, and problems will occur. An extreme amount of pride may cause self-centeredness or "big shotism." An extreme amount of greed may cause theft. An extreme amount of lust may cause sexual harassment complaints. An extreme amount of envy may cause lower production because the person is always looking at what everyone else in the organization has and is doing, rather than looking at his or her own work. An extreme amount of gluttony may lead to theft or disorganization, and an extreme amount of anger may cause an excess of complaints, grievances, unfair labor practices, confrontation, or drama. An extreme amount of sloth may cause an unsafe workplace and disorderly work areas.

Functioning alcoholics may be common in a workplace. Many alcoholics learn to handle both their jobs and their drinking, and this behavior can go on for years, even decades. This may be your more stable worker but not for the long run. They have learned and adapted to overcoming their extremes and their reactive personality character defects. They are generally good workers, managers, and executives. They may be, on the other hand, unpredictable and usually inconsistent. They can go for long periods of time without taking time off from work or being late. But in the long run, there will be periodic lapses of behavior that is unlike them.

They may go into periods of sickness or tardiness. There will be more than the usual doctors' appointments, and sick leave days will usually be higher than average. In the long run, the alcoholics' personalities and bodies will fail them, and once the physical or mental problems start, they will spiral downward for periods and then level off, only to come back worse later. This succession of events will continue throughout the employees' career until there is usually a total breakdown. There are some alcoholics who continue this pattern throughout their career into retirement, only to die a short time afterward. Once retirement sets in and alcoholics have all their work hours now free, that is an opportunity for more drinking, and it's usually this freedom to drink more often that kills the alcoholic within a few years.

If you've ever had the opportunity to see a long-time established organization, you'll notice that many employees who have survived drinking for twenty or more years and are close to retirement sometimes don't make it and die within a few years before retirement. Alcohol is a progressive disease, never getting better, and the amount of consumption is always increasing at a very slow, subtle pace, unbeknownst to the alcoholic.

There are identifiable characteristics of alcoholics. Keep in mind that many nondrinking people may possess some of the same characteristics. Alcoholics may be subtle, defiant, reactive, self-centered, controlling, perfectionistic, extremely giving, thrifty, nice, depressed, loud, boisterous, and involved with self. Many times they are perceived as liars, thieves, and manipulators. Alcoholics aren't truthful with themselves, and they become easily confused about what they said yesterday compared to today. Their minds teeter back and forth between drinking and not drinking, right and wrong.

Alcoholics are great pleasure seekers in everything they do; they are constantly looking for greater pleasure. They drink alcohol to overcome deficiencies in their personalities; it allows them to be the opposite of what they are or more of what they are not. For example, alcohol can provide courage where there is little. It can make a person more sociable and outgoing, when really the person is on the quiet and shy side. Alcohol may make a timid person boisterous or a quiet person loud. Alcohol makes the weak person brave and the unhappy person happy. No wonder alcohol is popular if it can do all of this.

Alcoholics can be very thrifty, or they can be the most giving individuals around, because of overcompensation and the guilt of spending too much on drinking. All alcoholics start getting some guilt as soon as they very subtly start to realize how much they are spending on alcohol and not on their family. Stopping alcohol isn't an answer in the beginning, but controlled drinking is the justifiable answer. After a while, even control no longer works; then denial and guilt start to set in, and things start to become unmanageable.

In the workplace, alcoholics may not stand out from other employees, because in the beginning there are few slipups unless they are blatantly drinking during working hours. The attitude of the owner or your upper management will determine the atmosphere of the workforce. Many alcoholics are what are called "functioning alcoholics"; they seem to perform their job quite well, no matter how much they drink after work.

Alcoholics are very sensitive people; they have sensitive personalities caused by exaggerated instincts, and they are easily hurt or offended. This hurt stems from a mind that is usually in a fog, and the mind compensates for this lowered awareness. Reacting is the most common technique of most alcoholics, since they react to the slightest negative verbal insinuation. They take everything personally and out of context in a subtle manner. They can have very sharp tongues they have learned how to use to protect themselves from any verbal or physical harm. They can put people down in an instant and have no remorse; they are always justified by their actions.

Financially, alcoholics are generally either in the low economic scale or in the high scale. To have enough money to support this habit, they must be smart; they must earn enough money to support families, kids, and a habit. If they cannot do this, they are usually in the low financial scale rather quickly, spending a good portion of their income on alcohol, and generally they stay there until the drinking ceases due to change, hospitalization, jail, or death.

A functional alcoholic can be hypersensitive to criticism. As an employer, don't jump to conclusions if one of your employees is hypersensitive but look for a combination of symptoms that could indicate a potential alcohol problem. Always keep in mind that an issue has to be related to work performance.

Many alcoholics can work hard, because they have extremes in their personalities. They are hard workers, players, and drinkers. Everything they do is usually to the extreme.

Alcoholics in the workplace have a greater need for attention, power, and control; and they usually have a case of "big shotism" no matter what their position is.

Many alcoholics can function quite well for a long period without any noticeable work-related problems; most, however, cannot.

Alcohol-Related Workplace Liabilities and Risks

Lower productivity is usually a good indicator of a problem, especially if the employer has provided all the tools and necessary training to do the job. Lower productivity will remain an issue and fluctuate like a roller coaster until the real cause of the problem is addressed. Alcoholics will consistently tell you what you want to hear.

Limits and boundaries usually don't exist for the alcoholic. They already operate at extreme levels on many issues; they will cross the line whenever it serves their purpose. This will lead to problems with sexual harassment, grievances, and unfair labor practices as well as an increase in union contract-related complaints. Limits and boundaries will be crossed in areas of work time, break time, lunchtime, interactions with people and with management, quality, production, ethics, policies, or procedures. And issues will happen time and again.

Alcohol is a depressant. The alcoholic doesn't drink to become depressed but to do the total opposite—to be social, happy, and relieved of problems and responsibilities. It's after the drinking has occurred that depression will set in. Many alcoholics may already have what is called a "depressive personality." Add some alcohol, and they become happy; then depression and anger start to set in. And then the next day they become more depressed than they already were. And this is the way it goes, day after day. The opposite of this pattern would be for them to recognize they are depressed and then do things to correct that feeling, not do things that will enhance it. This also brings about lowered self-esteem. When you have all this occurring at the same time in any given day, it may lead to lower productivity, decreased quality, accidents in the workplace, unethical behavior, or bad decisions. This depression will carry out to all the dealings an employee has with other employees, the public, or customers.

The employer will expend a higher cost to alcoholics in terms of leave, lost work time, claims, sickness, less production, lower quality of work, cost of terminations, and replacement. Then there are subtler costs associated with grievances, employee morale, and lost time to settle employee problems and disputes.

As a manager, you cannot change alcoholics. You can't fix them; only alcoholics can do that for themselves. Alcoholics must want to help themselves. In business terms, the manager will put themselves and the business or organization in jeopardy by making exceptions or lowering their standards of expectations. The alcoholic is already a professional manipulator. There is only one answer; if an alcoholic confesses an alcohol problem before termination, they have the legal right to seek medical attention to fix the problem. Usually employees will seek out counseling for a fixed period, thirty to ninety days; at the end of that time, employees are expected to perform at an acceptable level and eliminate the problems that caused the proposed termination to begin with. The employee is exempt from being terminated during that period when the counseling is taking place. There should be a get-well date that is agreeable to both the employer and employee. The managers' responsibility to themselves and the organization or business is to allow an employee to fix his or her medical problem.

As a manager, you don't have the right or knowledge to call someone an alcoholic legally or morally. Employees must use the word *alcoholic* as a recognition of their disease. Only alcoholics can admit it to themselves. Just because the manager says it, that doesn't make it true; the fact becomes true only when the individual says, "I am an alcoholic."

You can't always recognize an alcoholic in the workplace. Remember, everyone is at a different level of awareness in life. You will also have different levels of drinkers, who are at different stages in the disease.

In terms of alcoholic thinking, there will be a higher instance of accidents and claims. Alcoholics like to take on the victim role in many instances. Because their awareness level is usually somewhat impaired, they don't focus well on specific jobs or tasks, and they may be more prone to accidents.

Guidelines When Dealing with Alcoholism in the Workplace

- Focus on business goals, expectations, business results, and employee relations. As a manager, you can legally deal only with work performance issues when counseling an employee. You can listen to personal problems and show empathy to an alcoholic, but you cannot change him or her. As a manager, stay focused on employee performance.
- Focus on the issue, not the person. When you deal with the issue, it doesn't become personal. If the situation becomes personal, all objectivity is lost, and corrective actions will no longer be objective. Focus on the issue or principle, not the personality.
- Focus on suggesting ways to improve performance and behavior since they pertain to work guidelines and expectations. Alcoholics many times are defiant to taking and following directions and will function best by suggestions. When something is suggested, alcoholics now have a choice; if they are being told, they have no choice, and the reacting will start.

- Focus on not gossiping or making judgments of an employee. In a large corporation or organization, and in small businesses, everything discussed regarding an employee's work performance should be said or told in confidence. If an employee tells the manager he or she has a problem with alcohol, the manager shouldn't betray this trust of information. The manager now has a legal obligation to notify his or her manager of the situation. If you work in a pyramid-type organization, where there are levels of managers, the person at each level will have the opportunity to tell someone other than their manager. The information should go only to the lowest level of management needed to take action. It may need to go to the Human Resources Department or an organizational nurse. The fewer people who know about the situation, the better it will be in terms of employee privacy and morale. In many organizations two to three levels of management are all that is required to take corrective action. Practice a need-to-know policy.
- Focus on referring the employee to the nurse, employee counselor, or HR specialist, if your organization has one; and if you feel uncomfortable talking about it or dealing with the situation, a nurse or HR specialist is competent to deal with alcoholism or drug abuse. You can always refer employees to help lines, and counselors will usually do assessments for no charge.

Some alcohol programs can take up to four months to complete. Employees will need to provide signed documentation that they are attending regular and consistent counseling sessions, with a get-well date the counselor provided, agreeable to management. Alcoholism is a disease that can be put in check if the person is willing to do the work. Show empathy and concern in dealing with the situation, just as you would with any other disease.

Managers will always come in contact with employee personal problems that cause performance issues. Addiction in the workplace is a constant drain of energy and resources. As an employer, deal with performance issues caused by addiction and become a better company.

If employers are equipped with the proper information and tools, such as knowledge of alcohol and drug treatment centers and help line phone numbers, they may enter a win-win situation. Don't forget; you, the employer, have probably spent thousands of dollars training this person; you have a vested interest in his or her recovery, so help the person. It is cheaper to help an employee get well through treatment or counseling than to terminate and retrain someone else. If the alcoholic is able to recover and can get through one to six months of recovery, the employer will end up with a better employee than he or she started with. If alcoholic employees can lose the addiction and maintain the original motivation they started with, employers will end up with superior employees. An employer who takes the extra step will gain tremendously in the outcome of a recovering alcoholic. If the employee practices sobriety through a positive-living program, he or she will probably become a dynamic individual and your future leader in your organization.

This is the reason the manager must deal only with the work results and public relations, getting along with other people and measuring their production, accomplishments, or performance. The manager can list the deficiencies and suggestions for improvement but never identify the cause of a problem as being alcohol; if so, he or she may open himself or herself up to a lawsuit. The manager can probe the person for a cause, and once in a while, if the situation is getting bad enough, the employee might say he or she has a problem with alcohol. This would be the first opportunity for the manager to insist on getting documented help. Most alcoholics will be in denial right up to the point of termination, and at the last minute to save their jobs, they might admit alcohol is their problem. Sometimes employees know that once they ask for that help, in legal terminology their jobs are safe temporarily while they seek treatment.

It's up to the manager to watch for a slip in work habits or results soon after counseling has ended. In the legal world, employees get only one chance to fix their problem; legally there is no employee right to a second chance. This is up to the manger and the organization, based on policies and practices. Alcohol is a sensitive subject when it comes between the manager and the employee, and some companies will choose to downplay it. Focus on results, and if the expected results aren't met, then use termination.

Message to the Employee

If you are an employee being counseled on unacceptable work performance, you need to look into a couple of areas. Can you correct this deficiency on your own? Or with more training? If yes, then get the training you need and correct the issue.

If you are totally honest with yourself, maybe your work performance is deficient because of alcohol use. If you are being told you will be terminated if the performance doesn't get better, you have a legal option to correct the medical problem.

Before you are given a letter of termination or are actually told you are terminated, you have the right to tell the manager you have an issue with alcohol and would like to correct that problem. Once you notify the manager, it's your responsibility to seek medical treatment for the alcohol problem. You can seek medical treatment through a treatment center, counseling, or a physician. It is your obligation to provide the manager with documentation that you are now in treatment and what the get-well date is.

Normally a manager will give you one to four months to correct your medical condition.

As an employee, if you seek counseling or AA meetings, you will be expected to provide the same type of documentation. The key word here is the get-well date. You will be expected to return to work and perform at an acceptable level when you return from treatment.

Treatment may require you to be off work for a period of time. Counseling or meetings may be done during work or after work. You and your manager will need to agree on whether you will work during the treatment process. As an employee, you have the legal right to correct your medical condition within a reasonable amount of time and return to work.

An employee can request to fix the medical condition only once if it pertains to alcohol. If the medical condition cannot be corrected, you may be terminated. If you go to treatment or counseling, correct the medical condition, and still cannot maintain an acceptable level of performance, you may expect to be terminated.

As an employee, the best service you can give to yourself and your employer is to correct the alcohol use. If alcohol causes you problems, then alcohol *is* the problem. If you still cannot live without alcohol, check yourself into a treatment center. Your life and livelihood depend on it.

Chapter 8

Final Words

Society has an unforgiving labeling and judgmental process. Forty years ago, drinking was a manly thing to do, tolerated by spouses. Law enforcement tolerated drinking and driving. Today public intoxication and drinking and driving are crimes, subject to court punishment, public viewing, humiliation, fines, and fees. Nondrinking spouses today have a very high awareness level about alcohol, alcohol in the family, and verbal and spousal abuse. The word *alcoholic* still carries a very negative stigma in society, forgiven by many people but never forgotten. The amazing fact is that alcoholics participating in a recovery program are more aware today and realistic because they may practice a consistent positive-living program compared to the general public.

Alcoholics with one or thirty years of sobriety cannot walk around and call themselves alcoholics. "Oh, hi. I'm an alcoholic. May I have this job?" The word *alcoholic* describes a disease that hinders one's life goals, personality, behavior, tasks, and performance. Maybe this person less than, and is still associated with a brown bag, an unforgiving stereotype from society.

Alcoholics shouldn't admit they are alcoholics in day-to-day living before the general public, since nothing good will result from that. Unless alcoholics have a reason for doing so, walking around and saying you are an alcoholic has no positive purpose. It's hard enough for spouses and children to accept that word; don't flaunt it like you are important. It is a deadly disease that can be fixed, suppressed, or eliminated but never cured. You don't have to be an alcoholic; you can be a nondrinking person. It is a choice.

Sometimes it takes something drastic or some incomprehensible demoralization to get drinkers to wake up and realize they have a problem. Drinkers sometimes get what is called a "moment of clarity." This moment, usually brief, is when alcoholics know they should stop drinking, that there is something wrong. Maybe they aren't sure, but the moment provides clarification to alcoholics that something isn't right, that they need to stop drinking. Then the moment passes as they have another drink. All recovering alcoholics can describe these moments of clarity in later years, since they stick in their minds. Some say these moments of clarity are revelations from God, or the moment of clarity is God speaking to them. If alcoholics act on these moments of clarity, they may live; if they don't, they may die. In a moment of clarity, alcoholics know the alcohol isn't good for them. It is causing them problems; it is killing them, and then they have another drink. This pattern describes the disease of alcoholism. Alcoholics don't know how to stop drinking; they can't stop and don't know how to get out of this vicious cycle.

Alcoholics live in their own world, in their own mind, oblivious to the world around them and their surroundings. The number of negative stories associated with alcohol is unlimited and goes on and on. All the information below indicates the incomprehensible demoralization alcohol produces, and the stories are limitless. All the stories below would not have happened with a choice not to drink. This is a simple one-second choice. Drinking or not drinking is a choice every second of the day.

Testimonials and Case Histories

Below are some true testimonials and alcohol-related one-liners related to the consequences of drinking alcohol. Alcohol has no limit to its humiliation, dysfunction, guilt, shame, resentment, anger, jail, or imprisonment. These are no-name occurrences, the purpose being to show the patterns and consequences of alcohol. The consequences may be as simple as a DUI, a divorce, liver damage or failure—or as severe as drinking and driving and killing one or more people. In all cases consequences will happen; they will be in varying degrees of humiliation, financial disaster, physical or mental dysfunction, and family deterioration. Another fact is that each of the events below affects all family members. Alcohol or alcoholism caused all these events below. These are normal events in a life with alcohol.

This section is written to show how widespread, broad, and deep the consequences go. They are so widespread that no matter what city you live in, read a daily newspaper and look at the Internet news, and you will see alcohol-related stories every day on the front page, whether it is a robbery, spousal abuse, a car wreck caused by a drinking driver, or a wreck in which someone was killed. Domestic violence, a gun incident, a robbery, or a fight many times will have some alcohol-related basis. Then you can look in the obituaries; what you won't see is how many people died from alcohol-related diseases.

The information below is public information and can be found daily in any newspaper in any city or state. The stories are infinite. This information is public information, so there is no confidentiality involved. There are people who have killed someone while driving drunk. Drunk drivers who have killed someone are sentenced anywhere from five to twenty-five years in prison, sometimes a lifetime. And then there is the large number of stories you never hear about, those that don't make the newspaper, such as divorces, mental and physical spousal abuse, job loss, sole car accidents, suicides, individual physical accidents, unreported rapes, sex outside the marriage, physical fights, and any and all of the physical and mental ailments drinking alcohol causes. The saddest results of all are the stories you never hear about that are related to divorce. Alcohol is instrumental in a substantial percentage of divorces. The same is true for mental and physical spousal abuse; alcohol is a major contributing factor in the majority of cases.

Below are some one-liners I am familiar with. All these stories are sad, and they are being listed only to show the incomprehensible consequences of drinking alcohol.

- Jumping out of a second-story building while drinking, the person landed on a pointed metal fence, which impaled him or her through the back. Today the person lives in a wheelchair.
- Killing someone while driving drunk, this person was sentenced to nine years in prison. He or she left a family behind to fend for itself, and then there is the family of the person who was killed.
- People receiving a DUI are too numerous to mention. Each DUI has an approximate cost of $10,000 or more.
- Drinking people who have lost a job, a house, and a family are too numerous to mention.
- A person was stabbed five times in an alcohol-related fight.
- A young person killed his best friend and permanently injured his girlfriend in an alcohol-related car accident. Currently he is serving a prison sentence.
- A person severed his or her leg off in an alcohol-related motorcycle accident.
- A drinking person pulled out in front of a motorcycle while drunk and killed the cyclist. The person was sentenced to fifteen years in prison and left a family behind to fend for themselves, along with the family of the person killed.
- A person drove his or her car into a city bus while drinking and driving.
- A person drove his or her car into a crowd of people while drinking and driving.
- The number of people who have gone to jail not just once but more than once on alcohol-related offenses is an infinite number.
- The number of people who have committed promiscuous activities, unfaithfulness, and sex with other inappropriate people while drinking is infinite.
- Divorces as well as damaged and destroyed families because of drinking are incomprehensible.
- There is a significant number of people who died just before retirement or right after it. They never got the opportunity to enjoy retirement due to alcohol-related diseases.

- There are volumes of people who live in poverty conditions all their lives, always trying to feed the addiction, until death.
- One person fell in a drunken stupor and broke his or her neck. The person spent fifteen months trying to heal his or her neck, only to go out and drink again.
- There are many lewd acts that occur because of alcohol.
- Go to any hospital in America on any given day and visit alcoholics, whose livers are failing. When the liver fails in the human body, the body can no longer excrete urine, and it builds up under the skin. These are extremely sad deaths because of alcohol.
- One person fell off a toilet in an apartment because of a drunken stupor and lay wedged between the toilet and wall for two days before being found. During those two days, the person also suffered a stroke. Because the person lived alone, two days passed before someone came to check on and find him or her.
- One person was playing Russian roulette with a loaded gun while drinking with friends and lost.
- People are practicing prostitution to support their addiction.
- The number of college students who die from alcohol poisoning is always on the front page of a newspaper in any given city; they die due to drinking too much alcohol too fast.
- The number of people who have committed suicide while drinking or died from alcohol-related diseases is infinite.
- With an increase in domestic violence and spousal-abuse awareness and cases in the last decade, alcohol has been involved in a significant number of those cases.
- Sometimes there is satirical humor in alcoholism, from the person who received a DUI ticket on a bicycle and was taken to jail to the wife who hit her husband's head with a frying pan in a drunken stupor and sent the husband to the hospital, to the person who danced on tabletops while drunk, or to the drunk who took all his clothes off in public. These may be good for a laugh, but they aren't funny because individual lives are out of control with a drinking problem, the disease of alcoholism.

All the excerpts above may be described by two words taken from the book of *Alcoholics Anonymous*. Those words are *Incomprehensible Demoralization*.[10]

All the above information indicates the incomprehensible demoralization alcohol produces, and the stories are limitless. None of the stories above would have happened if someone had chosen not to drink. There is a simple one-second choice. Drinking is a choice every second of the day. Not drinking is also a choice every second of the day.

Alcohol experiences can encompass everything from rape, robbery, incest, jail, prison, drunk driving, drunk driving where someone was killed, divorce, endangerment, assault, physical abuse, mental abuse, and domestic violence. The stories are endless, sad, but true; and the number of lives the consequences of alcohol have affected is incomprehensible. For every alcoholic story, there are at least an additional five or more people the consequences have affected: spouses, children, parents, employers, relatives, and/or friends.

Here is an estimated breakdown of a DUI according to the Court Info. CA.gov. This estimate will vary by state:

Fines, attorney and court fees: $4,000

DMV paper work: $180

Towing and storage (five days): $685

Alcohol awareness class: $650

Insurance increase: $2,000 to $3,000 for the first year, plus additional years

Plus, there may be a loss of income and the negative consequences of future employment and of having a DUI on your record. The consequences are

---

[10] *Alcoholics Anonymous* (New York: Alcoholics Anonymous World Services Inc., 2001), 30.

substantial, and this money could be better used for food, a car, or a down payment on a house.

Alcoholics generally lack social limits and boundaries. What is invisible to a drinking person or group is that they are disturbing everyone around them. A drinking group has the typical alcoholic thinking that the world revolves around them, that their group is special, exempt from any rules; they are in their own little world. Asking a drinking group to quiet down may cause resentment, revenge, or defiance; and they might get louder. These are the typical alcoholic character defects present in many drinking people at varying degrees. This presumption that they can "do whatever [they] want," and have "no concern for others," and see "[their] group is special, and having fun." This self-centeredness and defiant behavior can be so typical in certain groups of alcoholics. Alcoholics don't want to drink alone (many do), and their friends must have the same behaviors they do. This makes their group special and unique; as long as they are all acting and doing the same, this activity validates their behavior as okay.

The saddest results of all are the stories you never hear about that are related to divorce. Alcohol is instrumental in a substantial percentage of divorces. Family problems start to manifest themselves, and so do the problems with the children. The problems start out as normal and subtle, and then they progress in a subtle way to more and more dysfunction in the family and individuals in the family. Alcohol is the cause of the problem. The same is true for mental and physical spousal abuse; alcohol is a major contributing factor in most cases.

Message to the Family Member

If you are a family member of an alcoholic—a spouse, son, daughter, or parent—you are directly or indirectly affected by an alcoholic; there is a program designed for you. Seek out counseling or Alanon is for the nondrinking person or family member. This program will teach you about the alcoholic and yourself and about how to cope and/or overcome your illness of being around or involved with an alcoholic. Alanon and Alateen are variations of the AA program and are there with your well-being in mind. These meetings will help you overcome the indirect disease of alcoholism and show how you are affected. There is hope. I have provided you with the basic information and tools needed to understand yourself and the alcoholic. Most of the subtitles in this book are the same tools you can use to recover your wellness. Meetings will provide you with an awareness program you may use by yourself in your relationship with an alcoholic. Providing help for the alcoholic is the answer and will provide long-lasting lifetime benefits. Understand that you, the family member, aren't the alcoholic and that you like yourself enough to seek help. If you are a nondrinking spouse, the best help you can give an alcoholic is to support him or her through a recovery program.

Message to the Professional

There are many variations of the twelve-step program of Alcoholics Anonymous, but there is only one twelve-step program of Alcoholics Anonymous. Many programs will use variations of the twelve-step program; some will use less program and more spiritual or religious techniques. Some programs bring the body back in balance with the use of nutrition, supplements, or medications, but all programs and variations of the program will try to bring more balance into the five areas of life: psychological area, physiological area, spiritual area, career, and family.

Most treatment centers will initially focus on bringing the mind or body back up to the norm with the use of foods, supplements, or medicine. Most treatment centers I know of always refer the alcoholic to Alcoholics Anonymous meetings after treatment as a long-term, lifetime, outpatient therapy. There are many paths to initial recovery. For the long-term lifetime maintenance of the family disease, there are organizations and meetings for the alcoholic.

- AA (Alcoholics Anonymous)
- Alanon (for the anonymous nondrinking spouse or family member)
- Alateen (for the anonymous teenager with a drinking problem or a drinking family member)
- CODA (for the anonymous codependent person)

- NA (Narcotics Anonymous for the person addicted to drugs)
- SA (Sexaholics Anonymous for the person addicted to sex)
- Adult Children of Alcoholics (anonymous)
- OA (Overeaters Anonymous for the person addicted to food)

This book will provide you, the professional, with an awareness needed in your indirect association with the alcoholic. Provided in this book is all the necessary information and tools needed in your professional interactions with alcoholics. If you are a professional, can you provide alcoholics with some help rather than just punishment? Some acts deserve punishment, but help for a person with a disease may lessen the need for future punishment. The benefits of help will always outweigh punishment.

Message to the Alcoholic

If you are an alcoholic still suffering from the disease of alcoholism, only two items are required to start recovery: a willingness to learn something new and a desire to stop drinking. If you have willingness and desire, you can overcome alcoholism. Acknowledge that you have a problem, a disease, because you cannot fix what you don't acknowledge. Find a higher power or God; this will be the extra strength you need to overcome the cravings. Seek out the twelve-step program of Alcoholics Anonymous, a treatment center, or counseling. Seek out a meeting in your local phone directory or on the Internet. This disease cannot be stopped or suppressed alone. Live one day at a time, get out of the past, and stop judging others. Be thankful for everything you have right now, even if you have nothing; be thankful you are alive. Get your thinking to the now and get out of the past. Replace all your time spent drinking with something positive, anything that will make you better, improve you, or reinvent you; learning is a lifetime job. What can you improve on daily in your finances, attitude, health, car, home, family, friends, and relationships? Strive to improve something every day. Pray, meditate daily, and ask your higher power how to improve yourself. Then take action; do things that will make you better. This next sentence will sort out those who will succeed and those who will continue to drink. For the first time in your life, like yourself enough to want to make these changes. Understand you are worth it.

Stop arguing about everything. Stop judging yourself and others and stop feeling sorry for yourself; move your thinking out of the past and into today. The maintenance and recovery of the disease are done with the help of a group of other supportive people; they keep you involved in healing yourself daily. This is a one-day-at-a-time job, because if you stop and go back to your old ways or thinking, you will drink again. Stay involved in helping others overcome the disease. Education is the answer to all problems. Live life daily, evaluate your problems, and fix those problems step by step. Both the person who hasn't drunk for one day and the person who hasn't drunk for thirty years, both are not drinking the same way; neither is drinking right now. And this is all you must worry about right now—not yesterday, not tomorrow. Find ways to improve your mind, body, spirit, career, and family. Improve the five areas step by step and day by day.

If you don't recognize you're powerless over alcohol or find a higher power, if you don't get out of the past or admit you are wrong when you are wrong, and if you don't give all your resentments, anger, and fears to a higher power, you will drink again.

The opposite of fear and anger is faith. Improve your faith, and you will gain hope. When you have hope, your faith will improve. There is a direct correlation between fear and faith. The more faith you have, the less fear you will have; the more fear you have, the less faith you will have. Fear and anger are the same thing. If you have anger, what is it you fear? If you are afraid, what is it you're angry about? If you have fear and anger, these two emotions will control your life, your thinking, and your actions. Give these two emotions to God and allow yourself to function in faith.

For the first time in your life, understand you now have choices. You now have the choice to drink or not to drink. Drinking is a choice you, the alcoholic, can make. You are the one who puts the glass to your lips; no one else makes you do this. It is your arm, your lips, and your choice to drink. Maybe for the first time in your life, you now have a choice to drink or not to drink.

According to Allan Hedberg, emotional intelligence would be the ultimate goal of every nondrinking alcoholic.[11] Be the best you can be. Emotional sobriety is the highest goal of every recovering alcoholic.

When the cravings come, eat sugar, drink fruit juice, read a book, pray, call someone, and meditate. The cravings will pass. Read the prayers below.

Based on my counseling experience, I am able to write this book so all alcoholics may have the miracle; all they have to do is ask for it.

I will end this book with a reminder of three prayers. Say them daily and when you need them. They will keep an alcoholic's mind where it needs to be. They will help you overcome the cravings and provide you with serenity.

Serenity Prayer (see chapter 4)

St. Francis Prayer (see chapter 4)

The Lord's Prayer

> Our Father, who art in heaven,
> Hallowed be thy name.
> Thy Kingdom come, thy will be done,
> On earth as it is in heaven.
> Give us this day, our daily bread,
> And forgive us our trespasses as we forgive those who trespass against us.
> And lead us not into temptation, but deliver us from evil. For Thine is the Kingdom, the Power, and the Glory forever.
> Amen.

---

[11] Allan Hedberg, *Living Life @ Its Best* (Bloomington, IN: Author House, 2013), 3–4, 53–54, 83–84.

If you are an alcoholic or think you may have an alcohol problem, here are some suggested short summary sentences that are keys to recovery:

- Admit you are an alcoholic. You cannot fix what you don't acknowledge.

- Stop trying to stop drinking. Just surrender. At this point you may need a treatment center or physician's care. Eliminating alcohol from the body may cause life-threatening events, such as convulsions, DTs, hallucinations, shakes, profuse sweating, or confusion. Notify your physician of what you are about to do and what medications you are taking. Prior to and at the same time you stop drinking, introduce nutrition with vitamin supplements of vitamin A, B complex, C, D, and E. If you are on medication, notify your doctor of your intended actions so he or she can monitor your state of well-being. The process may last days or weeks. When the initial withdrawal has subsided—and it will—seek out a positive-living program. Force yourself to go if you must; then if you really don't like the program, seek out some other form of positive-living program.

- Use a higher power as you have defined it. Use this power to overcome the cravings. Start on day one, using this higher power every minute of the day to overcome the cravings. It is you who decides whether to drink. It is your hand that puts the glass to your lips. Put in your mind that alcohol is no longer an option. Drink water, coffee, or soda until you have what is called moments of clarity or until your mind is clear and out of the fog. This may take days or weeks. During this time concentrate on nutrition and the healing of your body and mind to a more healthy state. Seek out counseling or an Alcoholics Anonymous meeting and try to go to as many as you can in a three-month period. The word *anonymous* is in the title of Alcoholics Anonymous; it is there for a reason. Use the meetings as your higher power if need be. Attend meetings and listen.

- All alcoholics experience fear, anger, guilt, shame, or resentment when they stop drinking. These will leave the alcoholic in time as the alcoholic begins to understand more and more. All alcoholics have experienced some type and degree of guilt, shame, disgrace, embarrassment, or humiliation in life. As the alcoholic begins to understand this, these emotions and feelings will also disappear.

- Purchase books on recovery or the Alcoholics Anonymous books: *The Twelve Steps of Alcoholics Anonymous* and the book titled *Alcoholics Anonymous.* Read these books every time the cravings occur. Get some phone numbers from trusted friends or people with some time in an AA meeting and call them with questions if you have cravings and before you drink again.

- In regard to the St. Francis Prayer: Generally, alcoholics are filled with shame, guilt, anger, fear, resentment, wrongdoing, discord, error, doubt, despair, or sadness. The alcoholic would rather be comforted than to provide comfort to someone else or to be understood rather than to listen to understand someone else, because he or she is self-centered to the extreme. The alcoholic generally possesses some of the negative parts of the prayer. The biggest gift alcoholics can give to themselves is to start liking themselves. Like and forgive yourself enough to want to heal yourself, to live, and to make yourself a better person. Sometimes alcoholics must make a 180-degree change in their thinking and learning. Start by knowing that you are worth it; you are a loved person in God's world. Start practicing the good parts of the prayer. Bring peace, love, forgiveness, harmony, truth, faith, hope, light, and joy. Bring comfort to others in need, understand the hurts and fears of others, and like yourself enough to want to make that change. You are the most important person in the world to you, and everything in God's world is just as it should be. Make that change and strive to become the St. Francis Prayer.

Let me summarize the suggested steps for recovery:

- Admit powerlessness over the addiction and get truthful with yourself for the first time.
- Incorporate good nutrition with supplements.

- Admit your character defects to yourself and another trusted person, and depend on a higher power to help you overcome the addiction and defects.
- Use a support group to help you maintain your sobriety and incorporate the knowledge of that group in learning how to overcome the addiction.
- Start to recognize the difference between right and wrong, taking care of yourself, doing good things for yourself, and helping others with the addiction. Do this one day at a time.
- Practice making good choices every second of the day.

Alcoholics must cure themselves by using the tools provided. As long as they do this, the disease will be suppressed, always ready to come back with the first drink.

Drinking usually starts out as a social behavior. It is the true addictive personality that will go on to become the alcoholic. Over two million-plus people have recovered through the Alcoholics Anonymous program. It is a successful program for alcoholics. The main book, titled *Alcoholics Anonymous*, is one of the most consistent long-term books being published today; it was published in 1939, approximately seventy-five years ago. It is revised periodically and has had the longevity and consistency to be a very popular long-term selling book with sales over twenty-one million copies. So something must be working.

Alcoholism is one of the saddest, most widely misunderstood self-inflicted fatal diseases in this country and the world. How many times have you heard the phase "Just stop"? For the alcoholic who loves alcohol and its effect, stopping isn't an answer. The answer is much more complicated, and, unlike other diseases where a physician may heal you, in alcoholism you must heal yourself. Every drink is a self-willed, self-destructive act for the alcoholic. My hope is that this book has provided you, the alcoholic, with the necessary basic tools to overcome the disease. The choice is yours and yours alone. May God be with you and keep you.

Appendix A

A Word from the Author

One of the greatest pieces of wisdom I have ever heard came from Fr. Bernie, who said, "When you have a problem, give it to God; when your children have a problem, give it to God." This wisdom will produce the best results. Fr. Bernie has passed, but his memory lives on.

This next paragraph is written specifically to the alcoholic; it is one paragraph directed to you, the alcoholic, a paragraph you alone will understand perfectly. If you are an alcoholic or someone with a drinking problem, this last paragraph is for you. This book was written specifically for you to save your life. This book is the last stop on the block. If you can't make it with this book, then you cannot make it anywhere. There are no more chances, no more excuses, no more lies. If you cannot get what's in this book, check yourself into a treatment center. Do what this book suggests because you are worth it.

Keep coming back to this book every time you get the craving; read it. Read like your life depends on it. Keep adding tools and coming back and adding some more tools. Deep down or in time you will know these are the tools required to stay sober. Speak the truth with no lies, no excuses. Here is the question: *do you want to live?* Speak the truth. This is a yes or no question. If yes, put down the alcohol, surrender, and read. Read like your life depends on it, because it does, and deep down you know it. You must be willing to do anything to get sober. Do this for you, because you are worth it. May God be with you.

Appendix B

Vitamin Supplements, Retail Distributor Information

Below are some vitamin supplement distributors of some of the brand-name products mentioned is this book, including their addresses and phone numbers. This information is provided to enable you to contact these companies to obtain further information about their products. None of the manufacturers or distributors mentioned have had any connection with the production of this book. Rather, we list these companies because we believe their products to be effective and high quality. Be aware that addresses and telephone numbers are subject to change.

Puritan's Pride

1233 Montauk Hwy

P.O. Box 9001

Oakdale, NY 11765-9001

800-645-1030

Puritan.com

Vitamins A, B, C, D, E, plus minerals

The Vitamin Shoppe

2109 91st St

North Bergen, NJ 07047

866-293-3367

Vitaminshoppe.com

Vitamins A, B, C, D, E, plus minerals

Vitamin World

105 Orville Dr

Bohemia, NY 11716-2599

866-667-8977

Vitaminworld.com

Vitamins A, B, C, D, E, plus minerals

References

Alcoholics Anonymous (New York: Alcoholics Anonymous World Services Inc, 2001).

Phyllis A. Balch and James F Balch, *Prescription for Nutritional Healing* (London: Penguin, 2010).

James F. Balch, *The Super Anti-Oxidants* (Landham, MD: M Evans and Company, 1998).

Allan Hedberg, *Lessons from My Father* (Nashville: Crossbooks, 2012).

Allan Hedberg, *Doctor—Teach Me to Parent* (Bloomington, IN: Author House, 2013).

Allan Hedberg, *Living Life @ Its Best* (Bloomington, IN: Author House, 2013).

Allan Hedberg, *Achieving and Living a Healthy Lifestyle in a World of Stress* (Bloomington, IN: Author House, 2012).

Caroline Knapp, *Drinking: A Love Story* (New York: The Dial Press, 1996).

Joan Mathews Larson, *Seven Weeks to Sobriety* (New York: Random House, 1997).

Frank Lawless, *Not My Child: A Progressive and Proactive Approach for Healing Addicted Teenagers and Their Families* (Carlsbad, CA: Hay House, 2013).

Gary Null, *The Complete Guide to Health and Nutrition* (New York: Dell, 1984).

Gary Null, *Gary Null's Ultimate Anti-Aging Program* (New York: Kensington, 1999).

Gary Null, *Gary Null's Ultimate Lifetime Diet* (Portland, OR: Broadway Books, 2000).

Timothy J. Smith, *Renewal: The Anti-Aging Revolution* (Emmaus, PA: Rodale Press, 1988).

Twelve Steps and Twelve Traditions (New York: Alcoholics Anonymous World Services Inc, 2010).

Grace Lee Whitney, *The Longest Trek: My Tour of the Galaxy* (Fresno, CA: Linden Publishing/Quill Driver Books, 1998).

Janet Geringer Woititz, *Adult Children of Alcoholics* (Deerfield Beach, FL: Health Communications. 1983).

About the Author

The Alcoholism Handbook is the culmination of my forty-five years of personal and professional experience dealing with the alcoholic, alcohol in the family, and alcohol in the workplace. I have specialized in counseling alcoholics for the past twenty-seven years, mentoring, counseling, and talking with alcoholics from every walk of life. I have dealt with men, women, and children as well as the professional person, working person, housewife, student, and homeless person, because alcoholism does not discriminate.

I have studied the disease of alcoholism, including its treatment, recovery, and long-term maintenance. I present to you, the reader, the best knowledge I have attained over those years.

I'm a graduate of Fresno State University, with a BA in psychology, and I have a forty-two-year career as a mid-level manager and executive analyst for a large governmental agency. I have twenty-seven years of specialized experience in counseling alcoholics. I reside in Central California (Madera), the gateway to Yosemite National Park near Fresno, with my wife. I have spoken at colleges, universities, and social and humanitarian agencies interested in this topic. I have traveled the country, speaking on the disease of alcoholism in many major US cities.

The information here is based on my experience and in-depth medical and experimental research professionals have published. All information in this book has been obtained from the public domain and the author's personal experience. *The Alcoholism Handbook* will save the life of an alcoholic and heal his or her family members.

Printed in the United States
By Bookmasters